A DIMDIM
IN
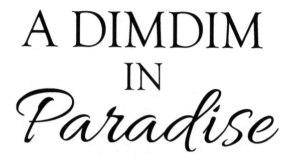

Thirty Six Years in Papua New Guinea

ANDY FLETCHER

BALBOA.PRESS

A DIVISION OF HAY HOUSE

Balboa Press books may be ordered through booksellers or by contacting:

Balboa Press
A Division of Hay House
1663 Liberty Drive
Bloomington, IN 47403
www.balboapress.com.au
AU TFN: 1 800 844 925 (Toll Free inside Australia)
AU Local: 0283 107 086 (+61 2 8310 7086 from outside Australia)

Print information available on the last page.

ISBN: 978-1-5043-2485-4 (sc)
ISBN: 978-1-5043-2486-1 (e)

Balboa Press rev. date: 03/11/2021

Dedicated to all the wonderful people of Papua New Guinea, including my Family in *Kopex,* Kavieng, Tembin, and Lae. A special dedication to departed friends David Loh, Peter Wakanga, Ted Whitaker, Brian Connelly, and Ken Burridge. Good friends truly enrich our lives Rest in Eternal Peace

Disclaimer

The names of many living people mentioned in this book have been changed, to protect the innocent and not so innocent from embarrassment. Some names of Clubs and Businesses have also been changed for the same reason. However, as this is a factual Memoir, it is how it happened.

Andy Fletcher Manoora 2021

Contents

Chapter 1

Bougainville 1970/71

I was born in Adelaide, South Australia, on the 8th of February 1947. My Dad died when I was very young due to Contracting Tuberculosis in the Australian Navy during World War 2. I was brought up as a Legacy Kid. My mother, older brother Jim, and a younger brother Rob lived with our Gran at Belair in the Adelaide Hills. When I left school, I did a five-year Apprenticeship with a Volkswagon and Porsche Agency in Adelaide. Halfway through my Apprenticeship, the Company was purchased by Ford. I played Football for Heathfield Aldgate United and Cricket with Heathfield. I also coached Junior Football sides. When I was twenty-two years old, I applied for a job with the Bougainville Copper and Gold Mine in Papua New Guinea in 1970.

After I had travelled to Melbourne for a job interview with Rio Tinto and was accepted, it was only a matter of getting my infectious diseases booklet up to date and acquire approval from the Australian Government. I would be on my way to PNG. But it was not going to be easy; the government refused to give their approval due to some trouble I'd had with the Police during my motorcycling days.

A visit to my first cousin (twice removed), *Professor Sir John Cleland*, the Brother of *Sir Donald Cleland*, former Administrator of PNG, proved fruitful. I came away from his house with a glowing character reference, written on behalf of his brother; this document did the trick. After much tugging of forelocks by immigration officials, I was soon off to PNG, aged 22 years.

Mum, distraught at losing her favourite Son, and being an experienced traveller herself, passed on her wealth of wisdom, *"don't drink the water, and always wipe the toilet seat."* Sage advice, especially about not drinking the water, which I took to mean I should drink beer instead, well!!!. I flew from Adelaide to Brisbane, where I had a 3-hour stopover, which I used to help acclimatise myself to the tropics, by heading straight for the Airport Bar.

When we arrived in Port Moresby, a hundred-metre walk from the plane to the arrivals hall and the heat radiating from the tarmac was stifling, and I, along with the other new chum passengers, started peeling off layers of clothing as we walked. Unfortunately, when we arrived at the corrugated iron terminal building sweating profusely, there was no respite there either. The ceiling fans seemed to just swirl the superheated tropical air around in a futile attempt to cool the place down.

As we had a few hours stopover to wait for the ANA flight to Aropa strip in Bougainville, an old hand informed us an icy cold SP lager was available just a short walk away at the Gateway Hotel. It was a pleasant walk through vendors selling paintings, trinkets and *buaii*, aka betel nut, a mild stimulant, chewed with *kambang* (crushed coral) and *daka*, a variety of pepper. This mixture turned bright red in the mouth and spat lazily on the ground or in bins and made the place look, smell, revolting.

I was, at that time, though, intent on getting to the bar, as I was nearly melting, taking advice from the old hand, I soon had an ice-cold *SP Green* stubbie in my hand. After the first one hardly touched the sides, I settled back in my chair on the *Balus bar deck* with my second beer and started surveying the surroundings.

I could make out the wartime *Jacksons field's* fortifications across the other side of Jacksons Airport through the heat-haze. In the foreground was a bustling horde of locals going about their business, occasionally flashing a brilliant white smile on their dark faces, their chatter interspersed with howls of agreeable laughter. Most people sat in the shade, greeting *"wantoks"*, that is, people from their same tribe, chewing together and seeking refuge from the scorching midday sun. I slowly recovered from the heat by sloshing down my third beer; I thought, *"yes, I think I'm going to like it here."* Mum had implored me to visit *Sir Donald Cleland* during this stopover. I felt a bit guilty that I had decided to drink beer; instead, I never did get to meet him, as he died in 1975.

One of our group informed us we better get back to the Airport, as our plane would soon be ready for boarding, so we unsteadily ventured out into the blazing sun, *"mad dogs & Englishmen"* springing immediately to mind. I needed a comfort break on entering the *"Men's toilet"* at the departure lounge. I encountered a strong odour of a not too clean urinal; Mums final words sprang to mind, *"always wipe the toilet seat,"* I chuckled to myself; this place needed an industrial steam cleaner through it. We finally took off, courtesy of Australian airline ANA, and a couple of hours later landed at Aropa strip on Bougainville. The airstrip was carved from a Coconut plantation and ran parallel to the beach. Everything seemed so green after the sunburnt browns of Australia; looking out over the shimmering blue sea to some small islands, I wondered if I would ever get a chance to visit them.

We were met and welcomed by Bougainville Copper Mine staff. And bundled along with our luggage and tool-boxes into the back of a truck. We then sped off along the dirt track through *Aropa Plantation,* passing smiling waving children, through roadside villages, and across crystal clear, fast-flowing rivers and streams. Evoking memories of *James A Michener* books I had read, I was excited at the prospect of living and working here. We had to wait our turn at the one-way section up *Kieta hill,* but shortly after, we arrived at *Kobuan camp,* not far from Kieta town. All the roads on Bougainville were dirt at this time in 1970, but that trip from the airport just blew me away, with the beautiful scenery, the local villages, and friendly, dark-skinned locals. We stayed that first night in *Bougainville* at the company *Kobuan camp.* After being allocated our *dongas* for the night, we settled down on the breezeway to drink a few more SP Stubbies in the sea breeze and admire the fabulous beach and tropical foliage.

The local staff at Kobuan spoke English to us but spoke *"Pidgin"* when talking amongst themselves; I made a mental note to learn Pidgin as quickly as possible; the howls of laughter from them as they discussed us made my ears burn.

I noticed some of the staff were very dark-skinned, while others were lighter, with red-skin and blonde hair. I also had seen the kids on the road waving at us were very dark-skinned, so I asked one of the red-skinned waiters where he was from; he told me that he was from *Rabaul* in East New Britain. I also asked him about the dark-skinned people, and he told me they were the local Bougainvilleans. He said with a smile that showed a flash of perfect white teeth; we call them *"sospan."* Enquiring what that meant, he explained about the black bottoms of saucepans cooking on an open fire. I laughed, happy that this fellow would share a joke with me. As dusk was approaching, the staff advised us our meal was ready. I later found out that the *"Sospans"* called other lighter-skinned Papua New Guineans *"Redskins."*

We had a quick wash and had our first excellent meal in Bougainville; The Company went to great expense to provide nutritious food for the workers. After Tea, we all adjourned for a few more beers, but the long day soon took its toll and had us heading for our dongas.

Kobuan camp was where everyone working for BCPL spent their first night in the territory; it was a dozen or so open-sided sago palm thatched dongas spaced out in a coconut grove on a hillside to take advantage of the sea breeze. It was just across the road from a lovely sandy beach, which had some small sailing boats invitingly on it. All the dongas at the camp had magnificent views out over Kobuan Bay. The ablution block was away from the rest of the dongas. It was at the end of a cement path lined with shrubs.

That night, as I made my way through the dark along this path for my shower, the rustling in the foliage along the trail, created by unidentified wild animals, had me jumping and recoiling from each noise. I had visions of exotic beasts and giant Anacondas, just waiting to pounce and gobble me up. The staff who was observing my not so Tarzan like behaviour were rolling about laughing at my antics; one of them called out to me, *"ol Rokrok tasol,"* Which I later found out meant it's only frogs.

After surviving my wildlife adventure in the Jungle, A staff showed me how to use the mosquito net back in my donga. These were essential items on all beds. As the dongas had no windows, and Bougainville, like the rest of PNG, was riddled with Malaria. Matches pushed through the net blocked any holes in it. After a final inspection of the net for any missed spots and tucking it under the mattress, I was satisfied that no mozzies could get in. Being such an eventful day, I soon dozed off to the mesmerising buzz of the mozzies circling my net, trying to get inside. The next morning I awoke, to the sound of mozzies still, only to find the net was full of them, all bloated with my blood, trying to find a way out. How this happened to me every time I slept inside a mosquito net in PNG, I could never understand.

In the morning after breakfast, we were picked up by a Manhaul truck and headed up the mine access road to *Panguna,* the rich *Bougainville Gold and Copper Mine* site. The road up was pretty hairy, with a cliff on one side of the road and a two hundred foot drop down to a raging river on the other. Looking out to the right, you could see the active volcano *Mount Bagana* spewing ash and fumes, and when we came over the range at the top, there was the mine laid out below us. Much building and clearing bush were going on as the mine was not yet in production. We drove on down past a post office and a bank. And up the hill to my first home in PNG, *Camp Three.*

Camp one was the biggest camp; it housed contractors working on setting up the Mine. Camp two was the BCPL Apprentice quarters. Camp three, my Camp, was for BCPL Expatriate Staff, and Camp 7 was for the BCPL and Contractors indigenous Staff. Between camp two and camp three was a Wet Mess. We had to attend the Administration block called the Pink Palace to do an Orientation week. We spent a lot of time learning correct ways of addressing the locals; racism was strictly not tolerated. Many Ex-pats were sent back to Australia because of breaches of this code. We soon knew how the locals owned everything, and if you ate a local coconut or banana, you must pay.

After Orientation was over, allocations to the four shifts at the mine pit workshop were released; I was in Shift two, the first day at the mine, all the new guys met the *Workshop Manager,* a vertically challenged Texan. He wore tooled leather cowboy boots and an oversized Stetson cowboy hat; unsurprisingly, he was called *Tex.* Tex told us they had a problem; they had too many light vehicle mechanics and not enough heavy vehicle ones. *"Who wants to swap over"?* he asked, looking straight at me, *"What about you buddy?"* I replied, *"stuff the trucks,"* immediately not endearing myself to him; Tex quickly dispatched me back to the light vehicle section. The trucks were gigantic *105 ton Euclid dump trucks.*

The first shift we did was a day shift; there was also an afternoon shift from 3 pm to 11 pm and a night shift from 11 pm to 7 am. We did all three Shifts one after the other, then had a few days off after the night shift, and started all over again. When the lunch bell went, I continued working the first day at work until one of the local mechanics came and told me it was *Belo Kaikai,* pointing at his mouth, time to eat.

I immediately started to pick up some of the Pidgin words, and during the night-shift, when things were quiet, I would get help from my workmates. I spent a lot of time learning both *Pidgin and Kuanua.* I soon

Bougainville Copper Mine Pit Workshop Circa 1971

became quite proficient in both *Pidgin, and Kuanua swear words,* Kuanua being the Language of the Tolais of East New Britain, who seemed plentiful on my shift.

One night during night-shift, the shift foreman came down to our section with steam coming out of his ears, *"Have you seen Bilson?"* he asked me, *"No I said,"* not knowing who Bilson was, *"If I catch that prick I'll kick* his *arse*," he fumed, storming off in search of him. When he had gone, out from his hiding spot appeared a young Tolai dressed in a bright blue cut shirt, with a cheeky grin from ear to ear; he asked if Wadey had gone. "Are *you* Bilson?" I asked; he nodded, laughing. It, was the first time that I had clapped eyes on Bilson, but he became a lifelong friend, *"He's looking for you,"* I said, *"what did you do,"* *"I'm not supposed to drive the big forklift, but I did and got it bogged."* he told me, still chuckling away. *"I would keep out his sight for the rest of the shift if I were you,"* I advised him, as he peered around the corner to see if the coast was clear, then disappeared.

After the shift, I and others would head for the wet mess where I'd down a few of my new favourite beers, *South Pacific stubbies*. They were known as *"Greenies"* from the bottle's colour; I would drink them for the next twenty years. Bilson was a Repairman, and he, along with the Apprentices, lived in Camp two under the watchful eye of the Apprentice Master. None of these guys were allowed to drink, but they were allowed to come into the Camp Two Boozer, buy soft drinks, chips, etc. They would each buy a can of Fanta, empty the contents and fill it up with beer, and when the Apprentice master would check to see if any of his flock were drinking, all he would see was a few of them drinking lolly water.

The way of the Bar was, if I bought four of my apprentices a beer each, then they would return the favour by each of them buying me four beers, I would end up with sixteen opened bottles on the table in front of me! Fifteen minutes after closing, security would come around with a big rubbish bin, sweeping all the empty and full bottles into it, no exceptions, a lot of beer went to waste in that bin.

During the day on our night-shift, some Ex-pat Tradies drank at Camp seven, the indigenous wet mess; this was because it was not far from *"Downtown"* where the post office, bank, and Store was. The other option was to tackle *Cardiac hill* and head up to Camp Three Boozer; we all decided camp 7 was more betterer. After a couple of months, I was drinking there once with two of the ex-pats on my shift, and I asked the Barman if he was from Wewak; he replied that he was; my two Ex-pat mates were surprised and asked me how I knew that. I found that though there were around 800 different language groups in PNG, and many worked at Panguna, I recognised what area certain people came. A couple of months after I arrived, the permanent accommodation, *Karewong Haus,* for the tradesmen. And *Karoona Haus* for the apprentices and Repairmen were built. We moved out of Camp Three.

At least we didn't have to walk back up the steep steps at the bottom of camp 3, known as *"Cardiac Hill,"* when returning from town, though we were a bit further away from the shops. In Panguna, it was either raining or dusty; in our leisure time, we had to walk everywhere, either we got caked with dust or got wet through.

For our four day break after the night-shift, one land cruiser was available for ex-pat staff to go to Kieta, Loloho, or Kobuan. You had to write your name down on a form on the notice board. So even though I put my name down every time, I only ever once got a car. The only other way to get down to Kieta was on a *Manhaul,* which went down every Saturday and Sunday during our break, driven by a mad Papuan named *Willie Moke.* The Manhaul was to be only for the indigenous staff, but they didn't mind if I came too. Usually, Bilson, Daniel

August, Jesse Poloat, and others would join me to risk life and limb.

Willie would get to the top of the Pass and then throw the gears into free-wheel and speed down the steep mountain road, with a 200 foot drop down to a raging river on one side. We would hurtle at break-neck speed down the range and on into Kieta; Willie, with a maniacal grin on his face, would ignore the pleas to slow down and the abuse hurled at him.

We would visit *Joe Tak Long*, Chinese trade store, and *Green and company* Store until 10 am came around, then we would hit the *Kieta Pub*. Lunch would come from the take-away, battered chicken wings, red sausage, or locally made pies. The hotel closed at 2.00 pm on the weekends, and we would spread out to the waterfront to continue drinking.

Sometimes the Police would come to move us on, and it's here that I found out about the *"wantok system"*. As the police were approaching, one of our group would always say, don't worry, he's my wantok, and after a chat in tokples by the two wantoks, we would not be bothered anymore.

I also joined the *Kieta Club*, as it was open all day, but I soon stopped going after I found out this club, like most in PNG at this time, operated under an *apartheid system*. The Whites drank, and the Black staff, demeaningly bare-footed and bare-chested, waited on them. My local workmates were not allowed inside. The trip back up the mountain to the mine was great fun, as we all were a bit drunk.

When we got back to the Mine, someone always produced a bottle of *Meri Buka* (Rhum Negrita), and we would sit up behind Camp Two, and later, Karoona Haus, with a music box, singing along to *CCR*, and *Canned heat,* getting completely shitfaced. Most of these nights, I would be too drunk to make my way back to *Karewong*, so I would sleep there in the apprentice quarter in someone's night shift bed and make my way back home the next morning.

When I moved into *Karewong Haus,* I got a new room-mate; *Merv Spence*; Merv, better known as *"Mushroom,"* was a Scot with a thick accent you could cut with a knife. He was halfway through *a round the world working holiday,* when he had got as far as PNG and never left, he married a Tolai girl, had a swag of kids, lived in Rabaul, and died from Prostate Cancer 2010. He was on the flight with me from Adelaide, and we became good friends, though he was on a different shift to me.

One day Bilson asked me if I would like to go with the Tolais on our shift, to Rabaul, on our next long break, to witness the first-ever *Tolai Warwagira.* He explained it was a big cultural show that went for about ten days, with sing sings, traditional dancing, and cultural displays. I jumped at the chance, and before too long, we were getting ready for our four-day break by sitting up the back of the apprentice quarter all night with *Meri Buka* and coke till the morning of the flight. I spent most of the flight to Rabaul throwing up in the toilet.

When I arrived, I was immediately impressed by the volcanoes and the beautiful scenery, the tar sealed roads, and the many shops and clubs. We booked into the Community hostel and almost took over the place as there was fifteen of us, I shared with Bilson, and he was to look after me when I became over-exuberant with the grog. After hiring a car from Boroko Motors, we went with a couple of the guys to Bilson's place at *Turagunan* near *Nangananga*, on the Kokopo side. Here I met Bilson's dad *Talele,* a Pastor, an impressive leader of men who built a church near the *Turagunan school.*

Bilson's mum also welcomed me with open arms and immediately cooked me enough taro to feed an army. Not being used to Taro, I couldn't finish it all, so I gave some to the dog, but she turned her nose up at it. Not to worry, though, as Bilson's younger brothers soon demolished the left-overs for me in no time at all. We went on to Kokopo and the Kokopo Tavern, then back on the Kokopo to Rabaul road around the beautiful *blue lagoon.*

We spent most of the days exploring the *Gazelle Peninsular* on the excellent road network, had drinks on the way and spent some time at Reillys Tavern. We saw traditional dance groups at the *Tolai Warwagira* during the day, the string and Electric bands during the night. And a lot of the day-time was spent at the Ascot Public Bar, or *"Boi Bar"* as it was known, one time I made a real mess of myself, so much so, I missed one night's string band music, I woke up in bed next morning with a sore head.

I got to know a girl called *Kelly Kinim,* who worked at the chemist shop. We went to the *Namanula lookout* late one night; I could hear the Malabunga high school band, *Pacific Vibration's* version of *"yellow river,"* drifting up on the frangipani scented night air, as we courted. The trip to beautiful Rabaul was over too soon, but I had fallen in love with the place, and it would not be too long before I would be living there.

Some of the Ex-pat workers complained about the Mine's wages and conditions, so they held a stop-work meeting. I told the conference that I had signed my contract because I was happy with my Contract. When I left Australia, I worked for *Maugham Thiem Ford* in Adelaide for $45.00 a week, and now I was earning over $100.00 a week on night-shift, with food and accommodation thrown in. I had come to Bougainville with a debt to my mum for my motorbike of over $800.00. I had already paid that off, so I was sweet.

The meeting also asked me if I could get the PNG workers to go on strike, but I refused; the only thing to come out of the meeting was to see if the crib-meals could be improved. A Crib was the cold meal that we took to eat at the workshop; I would get bread and butter rolls, salad, boiled egg, and cold fried chicken, which I thought was pretty good.

One morning after our night shift, we were lining up for breakfast; one of our Italian extraction Ex-pats started complaining about his crib meal, holding us all up in the line. He had ordered a steak sandwich. *"I wanna da steaka da sandwich, but it was a bloody colda,"* he said in his broken English as he threw the sandwich at the chef. All the rest of us wanted was to have our breakfast and hit the sack, and this idiot was holding us up. So I let fly, *"how in the bloody hell is he going to make you a hot steak sandwich?"* Crib meals had to be cooked prior to the shifts, *"do you want him to drive over to the workshop and cook it for you on a bloody portable grill."* I said.

The Chef thanked me, and our Italian friend went off grumbling about his *steaka da sandwich!* I seemed to get a bit extra in my crib from then on. The guys liked to play practical jokes on me, especially during the quiet times on the night shift; often, I would open my crib at dinner break to find a coconut beetle screeching at me. They would shriek with laughter as I would freak out. It was also common to find a piece of welding wire with *"kick me,"* written on a piece of paper attached to it, hanging from the back pocket of my overalls. *Willie Moke,* the driver, was one of those guys who liked doing this; one day, I got him back; he was leaning against the lube bay wall with his wire and note ready to put on someone.

I sneaked around the back of the bay. And through a hole in the wall, put a wire on him. I then came back out to see some of our crew sending him up; you can't get me, he said, as he was swishing his wire around. The look on his face was priceless when he suddenly realised his wire was bumping into another one hanging from his back pocket; the boys went wild with delight, rolling around on the floor shrieking and laughing.

My education in Kuanua and Pidgin was progressing slowly but surely; I had tried out some of my pre-learned phrases with some success when I was in Rabaul, I could now swear in Kuanua with the best of them.

Working at Panguna, I earned big money; I soon had paid off the debt to dear old mum, and the money was burning a hole in my pocket. There was a trade store at the town-site that sold expensive *Asahi Spotmatic cameras,* and I, like many others working at the mine, soon had a *you-beaut camera.* It had various lenses and filters; on my days off, I would be wandering around the mine and surroundings, photographing everybody and everything of interest. This camera didn't like the humidity of PNG and stopped working a few years later when I was in Rabaul. Another popular item sold at the store was the *"Panguna shirts"*, they were a paisley design, thin fabric, and very bright, with the two colour options being red and blue, or black and yellow. For years, I had a couple of them; wearing them in Rabaul showed everybody there that I had worked for BCPL.

The food at the Karrewong Haus mess was world-class; this was pretty amazing considering the Panguna mine's remoteness. Afternoon's shift at 11.30 pm, you still had the same choices as the day shift staff. One evening during a day shift dinner, we had a blackout in the middle of our meal; everyone groaned, then there was a hush. A voice from the darkness requested that the single ladies please return the candles they had borrowed, as they were now required. Howls of laughter erupted from the mainly male diners; fortunately, the darkness hid the single ladies' embarrassment.

At the start of the self-service queue line was a sign above a large bowl of Malaria tablets. The company would not pay sick pay if you came down with Malaria. The weekly preventative tabs were available free of charge. I did not get malaria in Bougainville, which was to come later in Rabaul. The company had its health centre, which had a big sign that announced that this was the *Liklik Haus Sik* (small hospital). I fortunately never had to visit it; they couldn't cure a hangover anyway, only time did that.

On one of the long break weekends after night-shift, Trevor, one of the Ex-pats on my shift, told me he had got a small Landcruiser for a couple of days, and would I like to join him and another guy who was a keen sailor, to do some sailing at Kobuan. Being from seafaring stock, I thought I would give it a go, so we set off for the one hour trip down the mine road to Kobuan beach, across the street from the Camp. After getting a bit of help rigging the little sailing dinghy, I headed out into Kobuan bay, on a lovely day. There was a fair breeze coming off the land; this soon had me scooting along at good speed. The others, not being as experienced a sailor like me, were zigzagging, sailing much slower, and heading further out into the bay

In no time, I had arrived at the beautiful white sand beach about 3 kilometres across the bay from Kobuan, so I er *parked* the dinghy and went and had a bit of a look around. I thought this place would be an excellent place for a picnic, adequate shade, fabulous beach, and secluded; after a while, feeling thirsty, I decided to return to Kobuan. I thought this might be more difficult, as I had a *headwind*, I pushed the boat out into the deeper water to give me a chance to get going, aimed the pointy end towards Kobuan, jumped in, turned the tiller for the quickest way back home, but just went back onto the beach. After a half a dozen fruitless attempts, the rescue boat guys, who had been watching my displays of seamanship from over at Kobuan beach. They came out to me in the rescue boat; they told me I had to *Tack into the wind*; I stared blankly back at them and shrugged, indicating I had no clue what they were talking about, so I had to suffer the embarrassment of being towed back into Kobuan.

My colleagues had finished with their sailing and already tossed down some coldies. When they towed me in, I had to suffer a good-natured barrage of derogatory remarks on my *nautical skills*, or lack of them, more correctly. That was the first and only time in my entire life that I ever drove a wind-powered craft, give me a boat with a motor anytime.

There were other times that I stayed at Kobuan during our long breaks; I could walk into Kieta to the pub or relax around the camp, practising my newly acquired Pidgin skills on the staff. One day I thought I would go for a walk around the bay with my new camera, to the beach where I had ended up in the dinghy.

As I walked past the dinghies in front of the camp, I'm sure I heard them sneering at me, or was it just the wind? Not far from Kobuan was a village where I stopped and took some photos. A local guy came and asked me where I was going; I told him in Pidgin, I was taking some pictures, which seemed to impress him, so he asked if he could come. As we walked around the bay, I quizzed him on the local landmark's names, which I was photographing. I enjoyed speaking pidgin, even though I was still making some blunders. He laughed when I made a blue, but he also corrected me. He told me he attended the Catholic High school in Kieta. He asked me if I wanted to come to the *Kapti Dei* (Cup tea day) coming up on the weekend of my next long break, so I promised I would go and support the school. We eventually reached the place where I had become stranded in the dinghy, then on a little further, and climbed up on the rocky headland for a great view and photos.

It was sweltering on the beach, so we went for a refreshing swim in the crystal clear, balmy water then sat in the shade of some coconut palms and chatted. It was only when a canoe paddled silently around the headland, carrying some elders from his village, that he bade me farewell and hitched a ride with them. I walked back around the bay for lunch at Kobuan, quite chuffed at my efforts at speaking Pidgin, being able to converse with a stranger, fluently enough, that he understood what I was saying. I did see him at the *Kapti dei*, and ran into him a few times on break weekends when I was in Kieta. *My Wanwoks* from the Mine would see him coming, *"poro blo yu, mangki sosapan, ikam,"* they would say cheekily.

Bill Jones from New Norcia in Western Australia lived in the room next to mine in Karewong Haus; he was an overweight friendly type of guy, great to have a drink with. Bill became a good friend of mine, but he hated Peter, my ex-roomie from Camp Two, as did most people; he would bait him all the time, which was a dangerous game to play, as Peter had a short fuse. One day as Bill was having a real go at Peter, he snapped and laid into Bill with a vengeance; he gave him a real hiding, my efforts, and those of others failed to stop him.

Bill ended up in the *Liklik Haus Sik*, but Peter was on the first plane off the island, so Bill was a hero when he returned to work battered and bruised. He grumbled about how nobody helped him. You did a great job by yourself. I assured him, but he wasn't sure whether his hiding was worth it to get rid of Peter.

Hard to believe now, but I was starting to get homesick, and as I now had all my debts paid off and had money in the bank, for the first time in my life, I was missing the sport I had played back home and my family and friends. So I gave notice to BCPL and headed back to South Australia. Sitting on the plane from Port Moresby,

I had second thoughts. I thought, what the bloody hell have I done? I had enjoyed my time in Bougainville, had got good pay, had many friends, and had learnt pidgin, what good was that going to be in Adelaide. I had tossed it all in because of some wussy homesickness.

When I got back home, friends had moved on, everyone was working while I wanted to hit the boozer, and I hated the cold weather. So I wrote a letter to *Boroko Motors in Rabaul*, where I had hired my car, on my trip to the Tolai Warwagira. They replied with a plane ticket, and I was on my way back to Rabaul, swearing never to be so silly as to leave PNG again. I was looking forward to getting back to Rabaul, remembering the magnificent network of sealed roads in the Province.

It would be 35 years later, through no choice of mine, that I would have to depart PNG with a chronic medical condition.

Chapter 2

Rabaul 1972

As we circled *Rabaul harbour* on final approach to *Lakunai strip*, we flew directly over the crater of *Tavurvur*; I could smell the sulphur fumes from the volcano from inside the *Fokker F27*. I surveyed the town and surroundings as we came into land, remembering that it was only a few months previous that I had such a wonderful time here with the Tolai workers from BCPL; now I would live here, and I was excited. After we landed, we all moved across the tarmac to the terminal; the smell of sulphur was almost overpowering. The brooding Volcano was the culprit; it emitted wisps of smoke, causing the ever-present stench of sulphur across the bay from the airstrip. Nobody else seemed to mind the rotting egg smell, so I thought I would get used to it after a while. Walking past the bins at the gate, I almost threw up, as they were red with betel nut *(buai)* spittle. Another thing I would have to get used too.

I was met by *Peter Cartwright*, the Assistant Manager of Boroko Motors, and driven into town to meet the General Manager. He called in the used car salesman and, after being introduced, told him to fix me up straight away with a second-hand car from the yard. I chose a *Valiant AP6*; the next stop was *Burns Philp* to purchase some sheets and pillows for my *donga*. Then it was back to the *Carpenters* compound adjacent to the workshop to see my accommodation for the next year; it was a duplex *donga*. I shared the kitchen and Bathroom with the Ex-pat panel-beater and had my bedroom, lounge/dining room, and a fridge. I entered through my lounge, so it was a pretty neat setup.

The workshop where I worked was just a two-minute walk away. The Community hostel where we had stayed previously was across the road. On the other side of the hostel was the *Cosmo hotel*, which had a remarkable history and soon became my second home.

Peter came and picked me up in the afternoon; he took me to the *New Guinea* and *Yacht clubs*, introduced me, and applied for their membership. He later moved to Mt Hagen as Manager. I received a phone call from him one day, telling me, in Hagen, he had advertised for a local driver with a licence, a local turned up with my driver's licence, trying to pass it off as his own. Peter asked me where I kept my driver's licence; I told him it was in the Sun-visor of my car, but I never locked the car, so immediately I went out to check my vehicle. Sure enough, the licence was missing; Peter posted it back to me; needless to say, that guy didn't get the Driver's job.

They accepted me as a Yacht Club member; they were not fussy who drank there. But the New Guinea club knocked me back, as I was just a common or garden variety mechanic. It was only four years away from PNG gaining Independence. It was not long after that; the

NGC started taking local native members. Following this, other riffraff like me were also allowed to join; however, I miffed at being knocked back in the first place, didn't join until much later.

In 1974 when I joined *Raval Vocational Centre*, I met *Bob and Nan Gilligan*; Nan was the NGC manager at one stage. After work, I would go with Bob and have a few beers while waiting for Nan to finish work. I had got to know many of the members, and one day after drinking there for about a year, one of the Committee came and said he couldn't find my name in the Members list, *"that's because you don't want me as a member, I'm riffraff,"* I told him. *"What do you mean,"* he replied, so I told him about filling in an application before Independence and getting knocked back. *"That was then. Now we take anybody, even people like you, see we accepted Bob."* I couldn't fault that logic, so I was happy to pay my fee.

Working at Boroko Motors, I went to work in the morning; it was down to the Cosmo for a counter lunch at lunch. Usually, an open-Hamburger, chips and salad, washed down with three green SP stubbies. After work, I went home for a shower, then down to the Cosmo again for tea, and drinks, till closing time at 10.00 pm.

One week I would work five days for $80,00, then the next would work Saturday morning, and that week get $95.00; I would live from week to week, writing cheques to pay for my lifestyle at the Cosmo; unfortunately, some times my cheques would bounce, overdrawing by a few dollars. One day after being scolded by the Cosmo Manager for bouncing a cheque. I stormed into the Com-Bank, furious that another cheque had bounced for overdrawing just a couple of dollars. I angrily declared

I was closing my account and taking it across the road to the Bank-of-NSW. That would show them, I thought, let them grovel and beg me to keep my account with them.*"Thank god for that,"* said the teller, *"let them sort your bloody overdrafts out,"* not the reaction I had anticipated. The Bank of NSW, later the Westpac, never once over the next 35 years bounced any of my cheques.

When I started work at BML, they gave me the job of removing an engine from a small ship out at the Burmah Road slipway. I had two Apprentices, *Tibu Malana*, from *Nangananga Village*, and *Nick Kavok* from *New Ireland*. The *boskru* (boat crew) of the boat also was on hand to assist me. The workshop manager, a Chinese-Australian, apologised about this job. He told me no one else would do it, and when I started working out at the slipway, I knew why. The temperature was about 50 degrees inside the ship. There were no Engine room floor plates. We had to balance on the two-inch floor struts, which were too slippery. About a metre below the braces was the bilge which stunk to high heaven and was a toxic mix of old engine oil, fuel, and god knows what else. Because we all were sweating profusely, it was common for spanners and other tools to slip from our grasp and drop down into the bilge; Tibu and Nick took it in turns to retrieve them. We eventually got the engine out with much difficulty by removing the wheelhouse; the last thing we had to withdraw from the boat was the heavy propellor shaft.

As the stern (blunt end) of the ship was hanging over the water, I got the shaft moving, and it shot out of its casing like a torpedo. When the boss came around at lunch-time, he was pleased we had removed the prop-shaft so quickly, "where is it," he asked, looking around, *"down there,"* I said cryptically, pointing at the sea. *"What the fuck,*" he said, "*just get it out,*" it took a large crane no time at all to get a sling on to it and have it back on dry land. I reeked of fuel oil for weeks doing this job; when I walked into the pub for lunch, people would inquire how the job was going; they could tell by the smell that I was a diesel mechanic. Boroko Motors had tried for months to get this job completed, but nobody in Rabaul wanted to do it, then; out of the blue, they got my application letter, and I was employed to do the job; no wonder they had been so nice to me!!

At work, I wore an Army shirt which I had purchased from Croydon & *Viggers Army disposals* on Malaguna road, with a felt pen I wrote on the Back, "*Wanpis Itambu,*" around an outline of my hand. Meaning "*keep away; I want to be left alone.*"

I hadn't been in Rabaul long, before I experienced my first earthquake, or as they are known locally as a "*Guria.*" When the workshop at work started rattling and shaking, "earthquake." I yelled excitedly, but everyone else seemed to take it in their stride; no one took any notice. The buildings were all "*Guria proof,*" so I became used to the almost constant shaking as time went by. There were exceptions though, one night after my usual session at the Cosmo, we were hit by a large Guria 7.1 on the Richter scale. I was in my regular alcohol-induced deep sleep when it struck around 2 am. I woke up from my profound sleep, all the lights were out, dogs were barking, and people yelling, and my room was bouncing around like a mad thing; I tried to get out of bed but couldn't, there was a wall in the way.

Confused, it took me a while to work out that somehow my bed had slid on the linoleum floor to the other side of the room from where it usually was, so I got out the other side of the bed and hurried outside. People were standing around commenting on how big the Guria was, but as they never lasted more than about thirty seconds, when it had stopped, we all went back inside to sleep. Not long after, during the daytime, we had a 7.3 on the Richter scale Guria; this was a beauty; I was driving our work ute down Mango Avenue, when it hit, I thought I had a flat tyre, so stopped and got out, and immediately fell. I looked up, and the power lines were whipping around above me, scared they would come down on me; I crawled out of the way into the middle of the road and waited till it stopped; I looked around, every-one was sitting on the ground.

I drove back down to our workshop, which was right on the waterfront; somebody walking on the other side of the road yelled that water in the Harbour had gone out. We all walked out of the workshop to look; we could see all the junk on the harbour floor as the water receded about two hundred metres. At that time, I did not know that this meant a Tsunami was imminent, but as I looked up across to the other side of the harbour where usually there was a line of coconut palms marking the shoreline, all that was visible was a wall of the water.

I thought, time to get out of here, as the water was coming back in, by the time I got across the other side of the road, the water was streaming over the road. I jumped in my car as the water was lapping at my heels; Tibu and Nick, two of the apprentices, jumped on the boot to give traction as my car started to float. I reversed out into the rapidly rising water, racing around the corner and up *Namanula hill* road to where the Japanese memorial now sits, and sat there and watched the sea inundate Rabaul town to about a metre deep.

At Boroko Motors, the latest model Ford Cortina had arrived just a few days before the *tsunami*; they were in a yard behind the workshop. When the tsunami struck, they had seawater up to their windows. They floated around in the yard bumping into each other; we tried to salvage them, but there was too much saltwater damage, and eventually, they were sent away on a ship.

I kept running into local guys on leave from Bougainville Copper, and I was requested to help with transport. One day a guy I knew quite well asked to borrow my car, against my better judgement I lent it to him, and that was the last I saw of it for a week, except once when I saw him driving down mango Avenue, I ran out to try and stop him, but he made out he didn't see me. Doing this made me cross, so I found out where his village was; he lived on the beach about halfway to Kokopo. One day I was informed, the car was home at his place, so taking Tibu as a bodyguard, we went out to his village in our lunch hour; no one came out of the houses near my car, which had four flat tyres. I removed the rotor button to disable the vehicle, and we headed back to work.

I got four spare wheels off a second-hand car in the afternoon and went out with Tibu and Nick. When we got to the village, the tyres had been repaired, but the battery was flat, from him trying vainly to start the car without a rotor. I jump-started the car, and we headed back to town with both cars; I never saw that guy again; he must have been too ashamed to show his face.

One time I bumped into a Panguna mechanic at the market, he was with a couple of his wantoks from his village, so I invited them home for a few drinks and lunch. Soon we were sitting in the shade of the mango tree at my donga, drinking SP and telling stories. I excused myself to prepare some lunch, but being still quite naïve in Tolai customs and culture, I thought they would like some western food instead of the *"boring"* root crops which they seemed to eat all the time, so I cooked lamb chops, mashed potato, peas, and beans. What a disaster, they ate only the meat shunning the western veggies, which was a big lesson for me. They unsurprisingly preferred the local food diet that they ate every day, and from that day on, every time I had people in for dinner, I cooked local food from the market, a classic case of learning from your mistakes.

From our entrance, across Mango Avenue, was a food shop called *"A Pal na Nian,"* this is where I tasted, for the first time, straightened and battered chicken wings. They were delicious, and along with the battered meatballs, and the hamburgers with the lot, they became part of my staple Rabaul diet. I also started going with my new found friends to town and village clubs, where the bar snacks were usually hard-boiled eggs, though some more upmarket clubs like *Seawall Club* had a delicious lamb flap stew. My diet was mainly liquid and came in a green bottle; I soon started getting nicknames like *Togirin* and *Tobotol* for my fondness of this brew.

A friend of a mate from Panguna, *Herman Tuit,* introduced me to *John Kuau* from Ramale village at Kokopo. Though already married, John was a devotee of the famous Tolai 626 dances, and he introduced me to them. These dances were in a *bombom banis* (coconut frond fence) deep in the bush near the host village. There was typically a small generator, a single fluoro-light, lots of warm beer, a stack of records, a pickup, and no women, except to provide some food to the very drunk males.

After paying the gate fee, you went inside and danced around, clutching your beer to the scratchy sounds of the pickup. You didn't dance with a partner, though you had to *"excuse"* someone, so you didn't go out on the dancing area yourself. I soon realised that the night would be more enjoyable with a cold beer and brought a carton on ice in my boot's esky.

If I ever was too drunk to get through till the morning, or if rain interrupted the dance, I would head back to the host village with friends to sleep at the *"village hausboi."* Ramale became home base on weekends, as I became very friendly with John Kuau, his wife, mum and dad, and brothers and sisters. Ramale was the site of a camp built by the *Japanese* during world war two, where they housed the White nuns from *Vunapope*. I spent many weekends exploring the overgrown caves the Nuns had dug in the side of the ravine down the back of the village to shelter from allied bombing.

They also constructed an ingenious chimney made from halved 44-gallon drums laid out from the prisoners cooking fire up the ravine to the village. The allied fighters that regularly flew over believed the smoke was from a village fire. I found lots of Japanese and prisoner artefacts, like a Japanese 3-star helmet, an officer's pistol, and cooking utensils.

One Saturday night, after drinking all day with John, Nick, and Tibu, we were heading up the pumice track to Ramale, with the rain belting down and the way looking more like a river. We came to a particularly boggy part of the road, where a creek crossed, and sure enough, I got bogged, not just bogged, but buried right up to the windows. We scrambled up the last hundred metres to the village and got soaked through; John left us at the *hausboi* to go back to his wife in his house. After drying off, I lay on my mat on the bamboo floor, thinking how best to get the car out of the bog in the morning. I dozed off to sleep, pondering that question.

The next morning I woke in the early dawn, with the obligatory headache, thinking of the task ahead of me to retrieve my car. At least the rain had stopped, I thought, as I stumbled outside. There was my car glistening in the morning sun, parked right there in front of the *hausboi*. John had rallied the whole village during the night in the pouring rain. They physically lifted the car from the bog and pushed it up the hill to where it now stood.

The overnight rain had washed the mud off the car; it stood there glistening in the early morning sun, just like a new one. When John appeared with a mug of tea for me, he thought what they had done was *"something nothing,"* but I insisted on thanking everyone involved. The next time I came back, I brought a couple of large rice bags for everyone who had helped out that night.

A couple of my Panguna friends had adorned the two front doors of my valiant with enormous stick-on Euclid truck numbers; they thought it would be funny to put "69" in large numbers that covered the whole door. They thought this was a great joke. However, the white police did not, and they ordered me to remove them, which I ignored, asking what laws I was breaking. They couldn't think of any, so they stayed on the doors until I took the car with me to *Bialla*. The vehicle was copping a fair bit of damage as I drove it on some pretty rough tracks around the Gazelle Peninsular. Although I was a mechanic, I only did rudimentary repairs to my car. When two brake wheel cylinders started leaking, I just blocked them off with ball bearings, and when my muffler kept falling off on rough tracks, I removed it.

On a Saturday around lunchtime, as I headed out for a session of drinking at some village. I had my foam esky loaded with beer and ice, and with a spare carton of beer in reserve, in my boot. I was hurrying along Cleland drive when a taxi shot out in front of me coming from the harbour. With my ineffective brakes, I couldn't stop, so *T boned* the cab; I had not done too much damage to my car, I hadn't even damaged my radiator. But my foam esky had suffered mortal injury; water from the melting ice was leaking from the boot. A police car arrived and quickly laid blame on the taxi, noted my two skid marks, and checking the firm brake pedal, concluded I had tried to stop with my effective brakes, but the cab was too close.

One of the Policemen noticed the water leaking from the boot and thought it was petrol; I assured him it was only water from a leaking bottle. He wanted to look in the boot that would have been incriminating, so I told him it didn't open; he finally went away after checking the leak was actually water. After they had gone, I opened the boot to find the esky smashed and ice and beer rolling around the boot; lucky the police hadn't seen that, as they may have changed their minds.

My car attracted an unroadworthy sticker for a loud exhaust because my muffler kept falling off, so I had left it off. I just got some iron filings and shavings of iron from the lathe in our machine-shop and jammed it up the exhaust pipe with a broom handle, which quietened the sound down considerably. However, revving the engine too much would blow it all back out again. I went to the police station and got a local sub-inspector to come out to check it; he went around the back as I started the engine and revved the engine to about 1,000 rpm, not building up enough pressure to blow the filings out. A white Inspector who had been watching from a window yelled at me to *"rev it up more,"* so I revved it again, *vroom vroom, "no, more,"* he growled, striding out into the yard. *"Get out of the way,"* he said to me, as he put his foot down on the accelerator *VROOM VROOM* went the engine, and blew the filings out all over the local policeman, *"get it fixed properly this time,"* he said, which eventually is what I had to do.

Back before Independence, the local police could not book the white people, and they had to go and get a white police officer, one time; as I was driving the workshop ute, full of celebrating workers who had just knocked off work. Two local police spotted me drinking from a police car, who pulled me over. The copper gave the crew and me on the back a dressing down and told us to wait while they went to get a white police officer; as soon as they were gone, I drove off!

At the time, a popular band on the Gazelle was *"Pacific Vibration,"* made up of teachers and students from *Malabunga high school*. They had regular dances at the school, which outsiders were allowed to attend; I would go because Bilson's brother *Morris Totil* was a grade 9 student there, and he would invite me to come. These were great dances, great music, and the kids keen to show their dancing styles; one of the *"Pamuks,"* (prostitute) in Rabaul, Lucy (not her real name), would often ask for a ride out to the dance. It was a long way from Rabaul.

Taking her was ok until I found out she was using the back seat of my car to ply her trade with willing students for their lunch money; while I was dancing out on the dance floor, I never gave her a lift again.

Morris would come to visit for the weekend and stay over quite regularly; one Saturday, when I went to Malabunga to pick him up, the students in the dorm told me he was down at the ablution block, which was away from the dorms.

I drove down and called out to him, and he came out; he had seen me arrive and had finished his wash, he stood by the car talking to me, as he put on his shoes when a friend of his came out of the shower room to listen to our conversation. He decided it would be appropriate to wander out completely naked, water cascading off his body and with his hands cupping his genitals. He was in full view of female students in the girl's dorm; he didn't seem at all concerned with the way he was. I told him he should put on a pair of pants, to which he laughed, and replied, *"what for, nobody can see anything,"* which was true! When he was ready, he strolled back to the ablution block to finish his shower. Hahaha, PNG *stail.* When I was first in Rabaul, the District Commissioner Jack Emanuel's death at Kabaira over a land dispute was big news. The government wanted to build a powerhouse on the land, against the landholder's wishes. The District Commissioner had been lured up a track and stabbed with an old Japanese bayonet. The white-community had to stay in Rabaul and not stray out to the villages. As this is where all my friends lived, I ignored this warning; I never felt threatened in any way as I always had local friends as "bodyguards," accompanying me anyway.

I received an invite to a wedding at *Herman Tuit's* place at Bitapaka, I was the only white face there, but I knew many of the guests. After a while, I noticed two muscle-bound guys dressed only in laplaps following me everywhere I went, even when I stumbled into the bush to relieve myself. I asked them what they were doing, and they told me the village elders assigned them to make sure nothing untoward happened to me.

They didn't do a good job, as I awoke the next morning with a splitting headache; I think it was the homemade distilled banana liquor variously called *Iawa, Jungle Juice,* or just plain *Jayjay* by the locals. I was later on in life to use *Jayjay* as the base for my fruit punch. My punch became infamous at Vudal Agricultural College's *Graduation celebrations* and the National Fisheries College Kavieng. Another time when I drove up to *Ramale,* an old Sepik guy who had walked over to the village from a nearby Plantation to buy betel nut was there. He called out to my friends in Ramale, hoping to endear himself to them, *"kilim em,wanpla waitman ia,"* (kill the white man). He got quite a shock when they turned on him and chased him out of the village, throwing rocks at him as he fled through the bush! They returned laughing, *"Man imas pekpekim trousis blo em."* (he must have soiled his pants)

From time to time, there were flare-ups between different tribal groups, usually between the local Tolais and the Sepiks or highlanders, who worked on the numerous Cocoa, or Coconut plantations. Once when there was one of these quite nasty skirmishes between the Tolais and Highlanders around Kokopo. I went to the *Kokopo Tavern* one Saturday midday with three Tolai friends for lunch.

The Tavern was full of Highland plantation workers, who didn't seem to be too bothered about my friends. A large group of Tolais had crept up in the long kunai grass on the other side of the road. They then attacked the Tavern with *"waians,"* the traditional Tolai slingshot. The highlanders immediately fled, but the stones kept flying into the Tavern. We had taken refuge under cement tables; I could hear glass breaking under the constant barrage. I told one of my friends to yell out, advising the attackers there were only Tolais inside the Tavern, which he did; the stones then stopped. The Attackers told us to come outside; we walked out, where I checked my car, which I had parked out the front; miraculously, it had no broken windows. The Tolai attackers came out from the long grass, and we walked with them up to the next corner near the sign *"Kokopo welcomes careful drivers."* We all then sat around, laughing and joking at how the Highlanders had fled so quickly.

About fifteen minutes later, two Police mobile riot squads from *Tomaringa* sped past us and pulled up outside the empty Tavern. The Owner *Jimmy Chow* had slammed down the shutters and fled upstairs to his house when the trouble had started. The Police jumped out of their land cruisers and pumped the empty Tavern full of tear gas. We could hear Jimmy upstairs yelling out for them to stop, but it was too late; he came running out with a wet towel over his face. From our vantage point, we watched all this unfold to whoops of laughter. Until the breeze carried the tear gas up to our position, it quickly moved us all on, not so funny now.

Most working days after work, I drank in the Cosmo Saloon bar where they served the counter meals and drinks. Most of the people who drank there were long-time residents. So after I had eaten, I usually moved out to the public bar, better known as the *"Boi bar."* They had a jukebox and eight ball table, so it was more my style, cold beer, good loud music, and eight-ball, with the billiard cue's added benefit being perfect for air guitar.

Many of my favourite songs I heard for the first time on that jukebox when I listen to them now, it reminds me of the great times I had in that bar, *"Mississippi"*, *"All right now"*, *"Baby blue"*, and *"Beautiful Sunday"* to name a few. The best thing about drinking in the *Boi bar* was that no whiteys ever drank there.

On a Saturday, I was with some *Taubar* guys, I was on my way to drop them out to Bitapaka, but I thought I would drop into the Cosmo on the way to have a couple of drinks and buy some take-away. My friends were barefooted, and as most of the whiteys who drank in the Saloon bar were racists, one of them snuck off to get the manager to come and kick us out, they were too scared to do it themselves. When the manager arrived, he saw that they were all barefoot, apart from me, so he told us that we would have to leave, which we were going to do anyway.

The real reason we had to leave was my friends were black, but he wasn't game enough to say that; they always found some other reason to get them to go. He then noticed one of the guys was relatively young, about sixteen, so he asked him how old he was; he replied, *"oh about Six,"* meaning sixteen, *"What, What,"* spits the manager, *"SIX, you can't come in here and drink when you're six."* I didn't make the situation any better by bursting out laughing; I repeatedly tested what I considered racist rules at the clubs and pubs in Rabaul.

One weekend after spending Saturday night at a 626 dance up at Toma, near where the Germans had their colonial hospital, we continued with my friends, eating and drinking until late Sunday. Late in the day, I headed home to Rabaul, though I had no sooner started driving when I realised maybe I was too drunk. However, using age-old tricks, like sticking my head out the window and dampening my eyelids, I eventually arrived back in town. Opposite the Palms Theatre, a track led down to my Donga

People were congregating at the picture theatre for the evening's film, as I drove in happy I had made it from Toma, in the state I was in, I suddenly had a rush of blood and decided to plant my foot in the loose gravel of the track. My Valiant took off under power, fishtailing alarmingly, and I crashed into the wall of our Spare Parts. Everyone from the Palms, including a policeman, rushed over to see what had happened. "*Yu mekim wanem*," (what have you done) the policeman asked me as I unsuccessfully tried to look sober. I replied slurring my words, "*Dishpla graun emi blo Mipla* (Boroko motors) *shaposss mi laik bamim kar lo ia, shamting blo mi.*". (This ground is private property, it belongs to Boroko motors, and if I want to smash my car up, that's my business). The Policeman thought about it and then walked away.

The next morning the Boss thought someone had broken into the spare-parts until one of the staff told him I was involved, and I was not at work as I had a dose of "Malaria," he came to my Donga to see me. I told him it was just a small miscalculation driving and I had clipped the Building and was sorry; he went away grumbling, not a happy Manager. I started accumulating many friends in Rabaul, though I realised I had no expatriate friends; all my friends were local.

As I lived across from the Community hostel, three of the tenants, *Darrie, Wasita, and Daniel Biang* would drop in some evenings for a cup of Pablo coffee. *Darrie* would later marry John Nightingale and own Agmark; *Daniel Biang* worked for many years with *Pacific Industries.* and was involved with many bands. I would bump into him at many of the dances and functions I attended, and we became good friends.

In my quest to find 626 dances, I travelled all over the Gazelle Peninsular's excellent road network. I discovered many new clubs, some in the bush, some closer to town, and pretty soon, I had a network of friends who would keep me updated on the upcoming events.

One time I went with many friends to the Kokopo show, a *"request a song"* stall was set-up by one high school. You paid them ten cents, and you chose a record from their list; one of the guys with me liked the latest hit *"American Pie,"* and he would go back time and again to play it over and over. Every time I hear the song now, it reminds me of the *1972 Kokopo Show*

A trade store inland from Kokopo owned by a mixed-race guy called *"Kai Chew,"* I purchased cheap Chinese *"Five Rams,"* batteries for my portable cassette player. The batteries went flat very quickly, so I had to ensure the person in charge of the music didn't fast-forward or rewind. Kai Chew, at first, would ask me if I was afraid of coming out on these back roads. But after a while, he realised I was never alone in my daylight and nocturnal escapades; I was always with Tolai friends. Hard-boiled eggs and navy biskets were a staple in every trade store, and that was my survival rations whilst drinking in the bush.

Not long after I first arrived in Rabaul, I joined the New Ireland Aussie rules football team. I helped by coaching and playing in the group, once again the only white face. The competition in 1972 was quite intense; even the local Tolais had a team, *"Matupit Brown Eagles,"* Most of the teams consisted of West New Britain players, Pomios, and Papuans at the various institutions in the province. The PNG locals were very passionate about the game, as were the supporters. During a match against a West New Britain team, I had bumped one of the opposition players quite hard, and as he writhed around on the ground, one of his *"wantoks,"* ran onto the field and made a beeline for me. I thought, here we go, he will thump me; however, he bailed out when he got all the way out to me. He could see he was alone, nobody had followed him out, and everyone was watching him to see what he would do. So he waggled his finger at me and said, *"next time,"* and ran back to the boundary laughing, to the delight of the crowd.

Most of the players also played Rugby League, a game I had never heard of; the New Ireland players were very skilful at Australian rules but would forget some of the rules, quite often confusing them with Rugby League rules. New Ireland was advancing up the ladder; we were winning many games. When near the end of the season, we came up against the undefeated Brown Eagles at Queens Park in Rabaul. The game would be a big test for us; we let them get out to a bit of a lead but slowly started to peg them back as our boys gained confidence. We were only a couple of points behind with about five minutes to go when our full forward marked the Ball in the goal square.

Great I thought, as I rushed in to calm him down and tell him not to play on, as they were prone to do. He took a deep breath and calmly kicked the ball right through the middle of the goals over the goal umpires head. We all went wild with delight but saw something was wrong, yes the goal umpire, who was from Brown-eagles, had signalled a point. Our full forward, dismayed at this blatant cheating, raced in to object by *"snotting,"* the goal umpire on the nose, he crumpled in a heap, and all hell broke loose.

The Tolai supporters of Brown eagles jumped out of their cars; some came down from the market; they just appeared from everywhere. Our players had discarded their jumpers and fled into the distance. Our full-forward, who was a local from Matupit, put his jumper in my boot, as I did, and we sat on the roof of my car to watch the entertainment with a cold post-game beer in hand.

Some of the Brown-eagles players I knew also came and joined us; by now, the oval was seething, our players were long gone, but this didn't seem to matter, as spot fights were breaking out everywhere. Some drunkard came up to my car and said, *"emi wanpla lo ol,"* (he is one of them), pointing at me. He soon got chased off by my Brown-eagles friends. The police finally arrived and fired tear gas onto the oval to add a bit more colour and movement. I walked around and collected the discarded jumpers as everyone started moving away from the tear gas.

The fighting continued for weeks; some New Ireland and Matupit houses burned down. Eventually, the two groups got together in reconciliation, and with some compensation by both parties, the affair was finally over. The AFL season brought to a premature end, the league deciding to cancel the rest of the games for 1972.

One of the New Ireland girls, *Tarpon Ioses,* was a regular spectator and always came to watch our team play; asked me if I would be her escort for the *1972 Frangipani Ball.* She was quite a beauty and wanted a handsome, athletic guy, who could dance, as her partner for the big occasion, she couldn't find anyone like that, so she asked me!

I was a bit dubious having to mix with Plantation society; however, I could see she was petrified at the thought of mixing with all the white people at the Ball. So I agreed to escort her to support her and try and keep her relaxed.

We were escorted on the night by two expatriate ladies, one of whom was a Ms Kreepy, known locally as *"Kreepy Crawley".* As Tarpon was an official entrant, we had to have an escort; I don't know which one of us wasn't to be trusted, probably both.

A Dimdim in Paradise, The Author Rabaul 1976>

On the way out to The Ball, at the Ralum club at Kokopo. Ms Kreepy turned to me and said, *"It's wonderful of you to escort a native girl like this Andy,"* I was so embarrassed by her condescending attitude, she talked to me as if Tarpon was not sitting beside me. Once inside the club, Tarpon blew the opposition away; she was by far the most stunning and handled all the questions with ease; she ended up winning by a street. I liked to think part of her success was having such a cool partner. We had to dance a solo waltz, and it was all over. Kreepy dropped us back in town, and I took Tarpon out to her home at *Pilapila*; it was well after midnight when we walked down onto the beach through the bananas. The balmy night was moonless, but I could make out Tarpons dad, who had heard the car pull up, coming down the track to learn his daughter had won. I bid them goodnight and headed for home; I think her family was pretty chuffed at having Tarpon, as Miss Frangipani 1972.

It wasn't long after that I saw her again at *"PilaPila 1972,"* a music festival held at Pilapila beach spread over a weekend; I spent most nights out there, where I continued my friendship with her, dancing the night away.

One Saturday afternoon, a couple of my friends came around to see if I wanted to go to the movies with them, as it was a Bruce Lee film. Later on, Bruce Lee was a favourite actor for Papua New Guineans, joined by Jackie Chan and Jet Li. As the movie appeared to be a good one, I said I would go with them. The movie theatres in Rabaul at this time were still under the Apartheid system. The Palms was for the Whites, and the locals knew the local theatre close by as the *"Haus Musmus,"* (Bedbug house). The local theatre was where we went, the movie was great, and the audience, including me, got involved, yelling at the screen it was so addictive. *Kilim em....lukaut, lukaut baksait lo yu... pilim ah.* Great fun, like a pantomime, but it was stiflingly hot inside, even though the fans were going flat out. Despite the heat, I had never enjoyed a movie so much before.

Though I ate out most nights, I liked to cook at home; there were some excellent supermarkets in Rabaul, Steamships, Burns Philp, Carpenters, Andersons Butchery, and Rabaul Butchery. There were also many bakeries, and the Saturday market was great for fresh vegetables and fruit. My cooking to start with was pretty basic, but I soon learnt to take on more significant projects. I started experimenting with more local food, rice, *pitpit, kumu, kaukau,* etc. In the villages, I had *Aigir* quite often. Most of the ingredients in an *Aigir* was fine. However, I never could stomach taro much, and as it had a robust taste, it spoiled the taste of everything else in the *Aigir.*

A *Mumu/Aigir,* is where all the ingredients are wrapped up in a banana leaf, with Coconut cream, then put in a pre-heated pit, covered with hot rocks, then covered with earth and left to cook. When I went to *Daniel August's* wedding, Daniel was a friend from Panguna; I was so hungry when the *Aigir* was ready that I didn't mind the Taro's taste; it didn't seem too overpowering. Even coming across some fur on the flying fox's meat wasn't a problem; I just ate it all.

Boroko Motors began getting a bit peeved at the amount of time I took off from work with doses of *"Malaria,"* which seemed to coincide with heavy drinking the night before. So when I heard about a Japanese logging Company looking for mechanics to restart up logging project at Bialla in West New Britain, I went for an interview. They were keen to get me, the pay was a lot better than what I was getting, so I finished up from Boroko motors, though I did return to work there some years later.

I flew to Bialla from Rabaul in a Tein Otter Aircraft with my new Boss, Albert Stock. Albert had been working for Steamships in Rabaul; I knew him from seeing him around in Rabaul. He also was the guy who had interviewed me for this job.

Chapter 3

Bialla W.N.B. 1973

Bialla in West New Britain was where Japanese Logging Company *Shin Asahagawa* had purchased a logging lease from an Arab company named *Complex*. I had finished my job at Boroko Motors in Rabaul and headed to Bialla to a position with them as a diesel mechanic. The flight to Bialla from Rabaul took about forty-five minutes in a Twin Otter aircraft, and as we wheeled out over the ocean to land from the seaward side. I could see what looked like a very short unsealed airstrip running from the beach at ninety degrees to a coconut plantation at the other end.

As we landed, I could see that the strip covered in *karanas*, which is crushed coral, a popular paving material in PNG, packed down hard and smooth, is easy to maintain. A company land cruiser was waiting for me, and we were soon heading through the small hamlet of *Ewasse*, which had a Trade Store, an Aid post, a Primary School, Airmans Memorial School, a few sago leaf huts and not much else. A short time later, we drove past the big Machinery workshop and a few hundred yards to the camp, made up of ATCO demountable dongas on a grassy area right on the beach.

I was taken in to meet the camp manager and allocated a small room away from the beach; I enquired about the much larger rooms right on the beach. The Manager told me that they were all taken at the moment by contractors, but as soon as one of them moved out, I could have one, which happened six weeks later. That afternoon I met the other staff, as they came back from their various jobs, and got stuck into a few cold SP's; I found out I was going to have a Landcruiser and a crew of four local mechanics. I would cruise the bush where machinery was operating and keep the machinery on the move by fixing all the minor breakdowns on the spot.

The next morning I was up at five-thirty eager to get to the workshop to meet my crew and take possession of The *"Bush vehicle."* We then headed to the dry dock in the virgin jungle, where all the dozers and Timberjack log skidders were parked, waiting for their drivers. My crew swarmed over the machinery, checking oils and water, replacing broken hoses, and getting all the machinery fired up for the new day while I headed back to the camp for breakfast.

After breakfast, as I headed back to the dry dock, on the road, there were lots of small kids in the school uniform of the Airman's Memorial school, waving me down wanting a lift. So I stopped, and they jumped in the back; They told me that there was no Passenger Vehicles in Bialla. When I went past Mataruru village, two kids, who told me their names were *July*, and *Tuesday*, jumped in the front; they also told me their two older brothers were Skidder drivers. When we got to the school, I had about thirty delighted kids standing packed like sardines in the back of the Land Cruiser.

This morning ritual, taking the kids to school, continued for the entire time I worked at Shin Asahigawa even though my Boss and the Japanese tried to stop it. The village elders were in favour, so my Boss unofficially agreed but told me to be very careful and make sure I didn't have a *prang*. As the company was ripping off the local landowners, they always tried to keep them happy. The next day, Tuesday once again jumped in the front seat, which soon became the norm. When he was on school holidays, he would wait on the road at Mataruru and would come with us on all our jobs in the bush; he became the bush crew's unofficial mascot.

When a Japanese log ship anchored out in front of our pier, we worked seven days a week to get the boat loaded with logs and on its way. After the vessel had sailed, the pressure was off, and we would take Sundays off. Almost every free Sunday, Matt, another young expatriate mechanic, and I would head up to the *Tiariu river* for a picnic, stopping in at Mataruru to pick up some of our workers to join us.

When I first approached the River, one of my workers told me the river was like kerosene; I imagined a toxic stinking polluted waterway. When I saw the pristine river, I was stunned at its colour and cleanliness. The colour was sky-blue, hence the reference to kerosene, and it was so clear I could see fish swimming on the bottom in the deep holes. Where we had our picnics, there was a flat area that you could drive right up to the river, and just next to it was a tree with a rope that swung right out over the water and a log that we could jump off.

Matt and I would purchase steak, sausages, and chicken from the Plantation store adjacent to our camp. *Mrs McPherson,* the Plantation manager's wife, told us that seeing the Company Supplied us with full-board we could charge the meat up to the Company. So we changed our order to include all the expensive cuts of meat. I never found out what the Japanese thought of this arrangement, as they never mentioned it. They also never knew most of the food went to the Mataruru guys. We took a BBQ plate with us and had a typical PNG BBQ, lots of fried onion, bread, sausage, fillet steak, and chicken. To wash it down, we had SP beer and soft drinks for the kids.

Matt and I would drive to Mataruru village on Saturday nights; we would load our gear onto an outrigger canoe where the houses met the swamp. The guys would paddle us through the waterways full of water dragons the size of small crocodiles. They would continually drop from the overhanging branches into the water as we approached, scaring the life out of us. Soon we would come out the other side where there was a sandbar, where we would drag the canoe over to get to the beach. It was a lovely secluded horseshoe bay with a big sweeping beach lined with coconut palms. It was the private beach for the Village and was landlocked; the only way to it was via the swamp

The canoe with a petrol pressure lamp tied on the front platform with vines paddled out to the reef. The Mataruru' guys had home-made spears at the ready; they would survey the coral reef through the colourful fish-filled crystal clear water, just a metre or two below us. They would point and dive in to return with a writhing crayfish of humungous proportions. They tried to point out to me the tentacles waving in the water from under the coral ledges that indicated the presence of a crayfish, but I could not see them. They insisted that I have a go, but I couldn't see anything despite them pointing to crayfish everywhere. Eventually, I spotted something. My chance to impress, I dived in and swam down two metres to the bottom, and with scant regard for my safety, I thrust the spear bravely at my fearsome quarry. Fortunately, I got it right through the guts the first time I had speared a giant black sea slug. As I surfaced triumphantly with my trophy, the Matururu' guys were in convulsions on the platform *"Hahaha Andy kisim pis lama, ooooo pilisss hahaha."* When the canoe was overflowing with our catch, we would head back to the beach. The guys were by this time shivering as they always dived naked. While the sea temperature was a pleasant thirty degrees Celsius, there was a sea breeze which made it a little chilly out of the water. The guys soon had a large bonfire going; the *Kindams* (crayfish) were dropped into a drum of boiling seawater to cook for a couple of minutes. We then lounged around on the beach scoffing fresh-caught, crayfish, washed down with cold SP beer telling tall stories and late into the night singing along to the boom box music. Did it get any better than this, balmy Tropical night where everything was so perfect, at peace with ourselves? Even though we were from different Cultures, we were blood brothers sharing this wonderful experience. These Village guys had little monetary wealth but had such a simple though fulfilling and happy lifestyle that I was envious of them.

The 69 car that I had taken down to the pier in Rabaul before I left finally turned up on *The Dangit*, the barge that made a weekly trip from Rabaul to Bialla. I drove it off the barge, and through Ewasse, people stopped and looked as I sped by, then rolled their eyes to the heavens at the prospect of this loud wreck of a car disturbing the peace in sleepy Bialla.

When the first Company log carrier ship arrived to load logs, it was a big deal; all the previous vessels were not Company vessels, as the amount of timber didn't warrant the large company carriers. The Japanese bosses asked us all to join them for dinner on the ship. We had to be ferried by our Tug-boat to where the large ship lay at anchor beyond the reef.

The headroom on the Japanese ship was only about six foot, so some of us had to bend over to get about. We drank as much Suntory whisky and cold Kirren beer that we could keep down; we also had a pleasant Japanese style *Kaikai*. The ship inside was fully air-conditioned, it was icy cold, so when we eventually went outside to be ferried back to shore, the heat of the night hit me like a sledgehammer. As the Tug manoeuvered into the gangway, I noticed the swell had gotten up and made it difficult for our Tug Captain. I felt quite green as I started tentatively down the gangway; the ship's pitching on the inconsistent swells made it more challenging to negotiate. The Captain of the Log ship, who was there to farewell us, could see I was a bit unsteady on my feet, so moved in to help me. The vessel was bucking around in the swell as the Captain tried to help me approach the Tug-boat. A large wave hit us, I stumbled forward with the Captain hanging onto me, and we both ended up in the water. We quickly scrambled back onto the gangway platform with the next wave, afraid of getting squashed between the two boats.

I apologised profusely for my clumsiness that unplanned dip in the ocean had sobered me up in an instant. My

Japanese bosses were horrified; they couldn't believe what they had just witnessed. I'm sure they thought I had done it on purpose. They fussed around the Captain which much bowing and apologising, glaring at me every couple of seconds. I was too busy jumping back onto the Tug, much more nimble now after my dip in the ocean. When-ever Company ships came to Bialla after that; the welcome-function was at the BBQ area at the Camp. So our Japanese Bosses had no further loss of face.

One Sunday, I was sitting in the shade on our Camp beach with the spare parts manager and a new pommy mechanic, having a couple of quiet beers. The pommy guy was trying to start a 15hp outboard motor he had found in a shed, attached to an aluminium dinghy. He planned to go fishing with one of the Japanese bosses, who was already sitting up the front. He had the boat in about a metre of water and pulled the rope pull vigorously; he stopped now and then for a rest and moved the gears back in and out to make sure it was in neutral. We were bombarding him with *constructive advice* on what he was doing wrong, which only made him swear more, while the Japanese boss was sitting impatiently up the front with his fishing gear, optimistically.

All of a sudden, the outboard motor started at full revs and in gear. With a burst of exhaust smoke and noise, the Pom was immediately thrown back over the transom as the boat took off. The Japanese Boss jumped up and started wailing and flailing his fishing rod around in terror; as he headed for the open ocean without a driver. The two of us on the beach, constructively, started falling about laughing. The throttle quickly vibrated back to idle. The Pom surfaced, thanking his lucky stars the propellor had not struck him. The Japanese Boss stopped wailing, as it now looked likely he may survive after all. The two of us on the beach were still in stitches, rolling around in the sand, with tears of laughter pouring down our cheeks.

On a Sunday, I went with the Kiap to visit *Fred Hargesheimer* at his house on the beach at the Ewasse *"Airmans memorial school."* Fred welcomed us and took us through to the Radio shack he had, where he kept in daily touch with friends in the USA. I asked about his wartime exploits which led to him returning after the war to build the school.

One day during the war, Fred told us he was taking reconnaissance photos in his P-38 plane over Japanese held New Britain. He was daydreaming and didn't notice the Japanese aircraft come up behind him and shoot out an engine. Safely he parachuted to the ground and hid from the locals, as he thought they were head-hunters. He tried to cross the Island, but the bush was too thick, he survived on freshwater snails, but his condition got worse. He was contemplating making contact with the locals but was still wary they might betray him to the Japanese. One day as he hid near a river, a group of locals paddled upriver singing onward Christian soldiers. He thought if they were Christians, he probably would be safe, so he showed himself to them.

They were ecstatic at finding him; they had seen him come down and were on the lookout for him. They took him to their village. Where for the next six months, they fed him, cared for him, fished with him, worshipped with him, and most importantly, hid him from the Japanese soldiers. Through the Australian Coastwatchers, he finally was rescued by an American submarine and returned to America.

He returned to civilian life, got a job, and married, but he couldn't forget those simple village folk back in West New Britain who saved his life. He returned in 1960 and greeted like a hero. Fred resolved to help these people more, so he returned to America to raise money to build the Airmans memorial school and an aid post, as well as numerous other projects.

He settled in Ewasse with his wife Dorothy; they were both teachers when I visited. Fred kept coming back to Ewasse, even after his wife died from a heart attack until he was 90 years old. He was carried through the bush on a litter to view the newly found wreckage of his P-38 plane. A legend to the Ewasse people, *Masta Preddy*, as he was known to all there, died in 2010 aged 94. Fred wrote a book called *"The School that fell from the sky."*

Many of the company's machines were pretty worn out; they had belonged to *Complex* before and abandoned by them. Two old Allis Chalmers dozers being so worn-out, they kept throwing tracks. One time one of them had thrown a drive-track and slid halfway down a mountain, I went and got Robin from Mataruru in his Timberjack, and we tried to slide the track on with the Timberjacks winch. The 1-inch wire rope was straining to breaking-point when I went in to see why it wasn't moving; the wire decided at that moment to break. It whipped right back over the cab of the Timberjack, missing my head by a fraction of an inch. Robin sat in his cab, looking back and shaking his head in disbelief that I was still alive.

I was doing a stint on night-shift; the day-shift guys couldn't remove a very old and stubborn bald tyre from our big log loader. When I came in, the boss asked if I could remove the tyre on my shift but had no clue how;

they had tried everything. When they had gone, I got another loader, picked up the wheel, took it out on the grassed area adjacent to the workshop, poured diesel on it and set fire to it. The boss came in the morning looking for it, to find a completely clean and cooled rim ready to put a new tyre on. He was happy but said he would not have approved if he had known, as he would have been afraid the rim would have buckled.

Another un-roadworthy ex-Complex log truck smashed into a coconut palm with a full load of logs when the brakes failed. The driver was pinned against the steering wheel by the cut logs on the back that shifted forward. I got our oxy-acetylene cutter and cut through the steering column; the loud bang the column made when it cut through showed how much pressure was on the driver's chest. Though, he did recover, having only a few broken ribs.

The chainsaw operators had worked out a new scam; they found that if they cut off one of their thumbs and then told the boss the chainsaw had done it, they would get K100.00 compensation; the boss had about half a dozen thumbs pickled in spirits in jars behind his desk.

Our fuel truck driver was a young Tolai, who looked about fourteen, though his licence said he was eighteen, his job was to drive to the dry docks in the bush and keep all the machinery fuelled up. When his tanker was empty, he would return to the workshop and refill from our main fuel tank. He had a habit of driving the 3 ton Isuzu truck up to the dock, then bump into it, and run backward. Thus reversing the engine running direction, it would speed flat out, with the exhaust setting fire to the air cleaner oil. So with the engine speeding flat out and clouds of smoke pouring out from under the bonnet, the driver would jump out and take off to a safe distance. Many times I would have to jump into the cab and decompress the engine to stop it. The driver would wander back sheepishly, and I would admonish him *"you bloody useless prick,"* to which he would reply, with a cheeky grin on his face, *"yes Andy, nem bilong mi, useless prick,"* (yes that's my name, useless prick) which would crack me up.

After working for about six months, I asked for a few days off in Rabaul, where I stayed at Kaulau Lodge. It was great to get back to the big smoke after living in the bush for a while. I found the Cosmo had closed for good. The shock at my leaving on the Cosmo cash registers was terminal, a sad day for me and the town. After a couple of rest and recreation days, I headed back on the MV Dangit's weekly run. Most of the passengers had to sit down the front with the deck cargo, but they allowed me to sit on the back deck. A consignment of a half dozen foam mattresses for the Trade store was tied together; this made a fabulous deck chair, and that night a very comfy bed.

I had my camera with me and took photos of dolphins, my fellow passengers and crew, and the passing coastal scenery; I also had enough cold beer for the dangerous sea-voyage, so I enjoyed a pleasant journey. When I awoke the next morning, the barge was coming into Ulamona to a breathtaking scene. *"The Father,"* volcano was erupting, with three bright red lava flows streaming down the seaward side of the silhouetted mountain. The brilliant red sun rising directly behind looked like it was climbing out of the volcano's crater; the contrasts of the red and black and the cloudless blue sky made for taking fabulous photos. I had run out of the film in the camera the day before, taking some pretty ordinary shots.

The Japanese let us use an old office building for a Club; it had a two-bedroom flat upstairs, so with a few modifications and the addition of a dartboard, we had quite a pleasant drinking hole. We did not have a licence, so we had an honour system, where you ticked your page in a drinks book and settled up at the end of the month. Though the number of ticks never matched the number of drinks consumed and selling the drinks at cost price, we were making quite an alarming loss. We decided to cover this shortfall by selling Black Market beer; we had refused to sell cartons to the locals on many occasions. As it was illegal. But now we sold cartons at three times cost-price and quickly made up the shortfall. The Kiap was also a member of our club; he turned a blind eye to our Mafia-like enterprise.

The Kiap, was a bit weird; I think he had been in the bush for too long; one night, he had a *"domestic,"* with his wife, so he drank all the alcohol in his house. He then turned up drunk, hammering on the door of my donga at two o'clock in the morning, for me to open up the club. As the next day was a 5 am starts, I ignored the very loud abuse and the thumping and kicking on the sturdy door, which woke all the other workers up. I was not going to go with him to open up the club and have to sit, and wait, and listen to the rantings of this Drunk. After a very long time he eventually went away, he asked me a few days later when I next saw him, why I didn't come out and open up, I told him I hadn't heard him *"knocking,"* I had the distinct impression he didn't believe me.

One morning as I headed with my start-up crew to the Tiariu River where the dry dock was, I came across a landowner roadblock on the road at Mataruru village. They had a dispute with the company for lack of payment of land-owner Royalties; they did let me through, so I went and dropped my crew off and headed back for breakfast, picking up school kids as usual. When I got back to the roadblock, all the Japanese, the Kiap, his policeman, and our white boss, *Albert Stock,* were all there, along with the truck carrying the machinery operators. They were in a heated discussion as I pulled up on the other side of the roadblock; the Mataruru school kids jumped on the back of my Landcruiser. *Tuesday,* taking his usual place in the front, as some of the protestors removed enough of the roadblock to let me through. The Japanese came over to me, apparently not noticing the thirty plus chattering kids on the back, and asked me to help with the negotiations; I told them that I wouldn't, as the Company was in the wrong, and that they should pay them what they owed them straight away.

When I came back after breakfast, the roadblock was still there; I sat and chatted with the people, they let me go and pick up my crew, and I went back to the workshop. The Landowners came out from the office and settled down in the shade to smoke; I went over and had a chat with them and found out they would sit there and wait for the afternoon plane to bring their royalties. After handshakes and smiles, all-round, I went and did some work in the workshop until it was time to pick up the kids; when we arrived at Mataruru, the roadblock was gone, and logging was back to normal. It shows what a little common sense could do. The Bougainville Copper project was brought to its knees by Landowner royalties, as the Company there only negotiated with the PNG Government and ignored the landowners.

At the end of 1973, I decided that I had spent enough time in the bush and headed back to Rabaul; I had to leave my car at Bialla as the *Cacao* price was very high, and the barge would only backload that. I left the car with my friend, the ex-Parts Manager, who had bought *Joe Moscov's Trade store* from him. The car never returned to Rabaul; I went and saw it ten years later when I was a Senior Lecturer at Vudal Agricultural College and came to the newly built *Bialla High School* to give a careers talk to the Graduating Grade Tens.

This group of students graduating included many of the small kids in grade-one at the Airmans School, when I worked at Bialla back in 1973, and they recognised me straight away. During question time after my presentation, one of these kids asked me, Sir,*"did you ever work for Shin Asahigawa?"* when I said, *"yes, I used to spin around to Baikekea, Gomu, and Mataruru,".* Immediately they all started yelling *"69, 69, 69,"* freaking out the headmaster, *Nigel Gregory*. The students followed me out after the talk, with much excitement, wanting to shake hands, and tell me their stories of how they used to get a ride to school with me.

Some students came with me afterwards to show me where Joe Moscov's Store had been; my car was a pile of rusty metal and weeds.

Chapter 4

Raval Vocational Centre 1974/75

When I arrived back in Rabaul, I planned to buy another car to replace 69, then go on leave to visit my dear old mum in Adelaide. So I went around to *Tutt Bryant's Car Yard* to buy a car and chose a Holden HR Station wagon. The car-salesman asked me what I did for a crust when I told him I was a diesel mechanic and had just finished up with Shin Asahagawa. He shot off to see his Boss; when he returned, he offered me a job in the workshop; I told him I would go to Adelaide for about six weeks and then return and work for them.

He said they were desperate to employ a mechanic straight away, as they had a backlog of engine overhauls on about twenty Daihatsu 2R engines. The broken-down PMV's trucks were clogging up the workshop parking area, and if I worked for them for two months to clear this backlog, they would buy my return airfare to Adelaide, so I agreed, postponing my holiday.

I was given a flat on the first floor, above the service station, and quickly overhauled the 3 ton Daihatsu PMV trucks. A couple of months later, I visited my mum, caught up with mates, and then returned to work for Tutts.

I had previously met *John Rakana*; he was the Principal of Raval Vocational Centre out on the North Coast of Rabaul. He had been trying to recruit me as a Mechanics/Welding instructor for some time. I ran into him one night at the Ascot, and he again started on about how they had plenty of students wanting to be mechanics but had no instructor. Could I please help him out? I finally relented and told him that if the Education Department were ok with it, I would be happy to do it. John organised a meeting with the Education Secretary, *Mr Harrington,* and not long after I had a job offer, which I accepted. There was no House available at Raval until the Deputy Principal, *John North*, moved out of his three-bedroom house into a four-bedroom one in Rabaul. I had to move into a three-bedroom emergency accommodation house at the back of the Education office in Rabaul; the house was high-set and had a lockup underneath. The Lockup had some lovely spare furniture in it, and fortunately for me, the key to the lock-up was on the set of house keys given to me. So I swapped my standard-issue wooden lounge chairs with some very comfortable large cane ones. These travelled with me a few weeks later up to my new house at Raval.

On the first day of my new job, I headed off early out on the North Coast Road to make sure I wasn't late for work. I turned off the main road on to the school's track; about a kilometre along the route, a large tree was down across the trail. John North, Bob Gilligan, and several students were sitting on the trunk waiting for me, so I headed up in their car while the students waited for the Works Department to come and remove the tree.

I was shown my workshop and classroom and introduced to my twenty students, who seemed very keen. John told me of the one hundred and twenty students enrolled; over one hundred wanted to be mechanics. John went through the curriculum with me and left me to do my lesson plans.

At morning tea time, John invited me over to his, and soon to be my house, to meet his wife and large family, the reason for them to upsize to a four-bedroom home. As I came in the front door, I noticed a couple of *"watchtower"* magazines, the Jehovah Witness church magazine, sitting on the table'.*"Oh, aren't this mob a pain in the bum,"* I said, hoping to break the ice in my new bosses home. There was an awkward silence; I then noticed stacks of these magazines piled everywhere, and the North children all dressed in *"missionary white."* I could feel my ears turning crimson as I realised that they must be JW's. John coolly informed me that they were Jehovah's; I mumbled something like, *"that's nice,"* while looking around for a hole to swallow me up. It wasn't long before John and his family moved out of their house in Raval, and I moved in with my ill-gotten rattan chairs to the spacious three-bedroom house.

Thomas and Kakatoi were the traditional landowners of the school land and lived just across the road from the main gate; I employed their daughter as my *"Haus Meri"* (Domestic). Thomas Junior was a mechanic trainee in my class. The School had its generator, owned by the Electricity Commission, to provide power for the school and the houses; the power usually was from 6 am to 10 am, then 4 pm to 10 pm. I had an electric fridge and a kerosene fridge of dubious efficiency.

My house had a wood stove that also heated the shower water and the whole house. I purchased an electric frying pan I would make all my meals in, using it as a hotplate for a couple of small saucepans. We experienced periods when we had no power; the generator was not very reliable. It was next to a very dusty dirt road, which used to chop out the Generator's bearings. When the power was off, we had several small engine machines to run the compressor and welder for my workshop.

As duty-teacher, I had to chase the students out from the dorms at 6 am; they had a morning work parade, a water pumper went to each staff house. The cooks allocated to the mess, where Bob would come from his place to scale the rations for breakfast, usually a packet of beef crackers and a cup of tea for each student. Other students to clean the ablution blocks, and the most significant group would cut the large playing field areas with their "*Sarifs*," a thin flat metal grass knife with one sharpened edge. The Sarif was swung with one hand from behind the head down across and through the grass, cutting it off just above ground level, the other hand on the opposite knee to provide stability and aim. The swing through of the *sarif* was similar to a low golf swing, and the students showed great skill in using their *sarifs*; it was also great exercise.

One night I was on duty; I was sitting in my lounge room reading a book; from here, I had a good view across the playing field to the workshops, classrooms and the dormitories. I looked up from my book, aware something was wrong; it was too quiet, no laughter, no guitar playing, nobody chasing someone around, just the natural night noises. I grabbed my torch and walked across the playing field to the classrooms, not a soul, over to the dorms, empty; where was everybody?

I went around to the mess, two cars were parked there, and the door was closed, I tried to push the door open, but there were bodies inside leaning against it, so I bellowed, *"Open the door."* My voice had the desired effect as the door opened quickly to reveal two Expatriates and two National strangers holding a church service. I told all the students to file outside and then asked them who they were; it turned out that they were some obscure Christian sect. I told them they could not just waltz into our school at night without permission and start trying to convert our students to their beliefs.

All of our students were members of mainstream churches, and I'm sure their parents would not be happy if they returned home after a year away at boarding school, following some weird sect. I told these people I would address the issue at the next morning's Parade, where I would inform the students they would have to bring a signed note from their parents saying it was alright for their son to attend the sect. The sect people tried to change it to the message needed if they were not allowed to attend, but I was not having any of that. I duly brought the subject up at the next morning's Parade and told our students they would have to bring a note back from their next weekend home if they wanted to attend the sect. No-one came back from their village with a message, so when the preachers returned, I told them the news, they were not happy, but I told them they were lucky to escape trespass charges.

I soon got into the place's routine; every six weeks, the duty teacher roster meant I couldn't go into town after work for a few beers; I had to be available in case of medical or other emergencies. The most common, being Malaria and suspected appendicitis, students were either treated at our Aid Post or taken down to Nonga Base Hospital, about twenty minutes drive away.

Sometimes the students would fake an illness so that they could go for a spin to the *"Haus Sik."* (Hospital) If I thought this was the case, I would declare that I would treat them with chloroquine on the spot; this usually had them recovering remarkably swiftly.

We had an English volunteer named *Broadhouse* who had the nickname *"Bull-nose,"* given to him for wrongly admonishing one of my mechanic students for not knowing what Bull-Nosed pliers were. Bullnose had a project to build a permanent *"long drop toilet"* to replace the nearly full existing one. He had his students dig a deep hole, then instead of pouring the concrete slab over the pit, he decided to construct the slab in the shed, and then when it had set, he would have all the students in the school carry the slab to the pit.

He had calculated the slab's weight and worked out each of the students would have to lift 5 kilos or sum such weight. On the day of the big lift, all the students were assembled with metal bars under the slab to lift it; Bob and I were on hand to offer *constructive advice* and see what happened. It naturally turned into a circus; *Bullnose* was trying to get everyone to lift at once, which was an impossible task; the slab went up and down, first one side, then the other. *Bullnose* was racing around, getting more and more frustrated, *"lift laddie,"* he would implore someone; we were in stitches at the chaotic scene. Eventually, he conceded it was not going to work, and as we trotted off to lunch, he was trying to work out how to roll the slab to the site.

On the weekends, the Tolai Students and the Town Kids would go home for the weekend, but the Duke of York Islands students, who lived too far away out on the Islands, were allowed to stay at the school. When I was on-duty, I would have to stay back at the school instead of my usual market trip and later to the Yacht club. So I would give the students the option of going in the school truck to town with me; they could roam around town, then meet me at the Yacht club at a predetermined time for the return trip. This plan only worked if all the kids wanted to go to town, but they usually did.

Bob Gilligan was the plumbing Instructor and lived with his wife Nan in the nearest house to mine; Bob, like me, liked a drink, so we would spend the weekends listening to the Australian footy on the radio whilst having a drink. We also showed 16mm films for the students and the local community; the Mess became the *Haus-Piksa* (picture theatre) on those nights.

We would hire a movie from Gregory Page in Port Moresby, then swap it on the illegal film-swapping circuit, which included most schools and clubs in the Province. We would exchange our films if they were not suitable for our audience; Kung Fu and Action films were preferable. Romance films was a killer. No-one would pay the 10 cent gate fee to see people kissing. When this happened during a movie, there would be loud *sssishhhs,* and suggestions to the heroine to *"sssish yu go, take off."* Films that were popular when I was at Raval, were the *"Billy Jack"* series, *"Kelly's Heroes,"* and *any Cowboy*, but the best of all was *"Enter the Dragon,"* starring Bruce Lee.

This film was new and sent to a senior public servant, John Alberto, I had made arrangements with John to show the movie on a Friday and Saturday night, and we had sent the *toksave* (message) around to the local villages. There was a large, excited turnout waiting, even before I headed into town to pick the film up. But when I arrived at John's house, something was wrong; It was a *"Haus Krai,"* *(funeral)* a large group of people were mourning John's death, he had suddenly dropped dead from a heart attack that day. His widow was not interested in giving me the film, as she was still in shock; however, after a lot of persuasions, and assertions from me, that I too would be joining John in the morgue, if I turned up back at the school without the film, that they let me take it.

The Gilligans and I had been given a puppy each from one of our students who lived near Tomaringa; mine was black, which I named *"Two Ring,"* in honour of the green SP bottle, the Gilligans called their brown one, Brandy. Two Ring got into the habit of following the *haus meri* but used to sleep on my back veranda near the kitchen door.

On Saturday nights, I started showing a film at my house to the D.O.Y. boys who had to stay the weekend, Bob and Nan would also come over, and often we would have a BBQ as well.

A group of a dozen boys from *Toboina*, and *Palnalom* villages, up behind the school, would also come down for the movie. They would sleep overnight afterwards, draped around the floor of my lounge, and head back home in the morning after some breakfast. They were typical village kids, dressed in lap laps, with their woven coconut frond baskets, and their *Pornok*, (what we in Australia, called a shanghai) worn, as is the custom, on their head, leather patch on the forehead, wooden Y piece handing at the back of the neck. The Boys had a distinctive odour of kambang and ginger, which my house and car both reeked of; I not only got used to this smell even now, it brings back fond memories of a happy time in my life. Expatriates getting in my car would comment that my car "*smelled of Tolai Singsing,*" I didn't know the intent of those comments, but I always took them as a compliment.

My house, on these occasions, had become like an extension of the traditional "*Hausboi*" in the village. I would seek every opportunity to improve my *Kuanua* (Tolai Language) and those Sunday mornings before the boys went back to the Village for "*Lotu*"(church) were magic for me. I would listen to their conversations in "*tok ples,*" interrupting when I lost the thread, waiting for the chance to interject with my contribution. Which thanks to my early lessons at Panguna, usually interlaced with a fair number of swear words, resulting in the kids cracking up, I always knew how to get a laugh. Toboina was on the road from *Iatapal* to *Putanagororoi,* on the North Coast, also had a drinking club, which I used to frequent regularly; it was the closest watering hole to my house. Though the beer was warm, I got used to drinking beer that way; in fact, there is far more taste in warm beer than in cold beer; cold beer is so cold it freezes your taste buds.

On a Saturday, I showed a film about werewolves, a Horror Movie, or as the students called a "*Frighten film.*" After the movies, the students would wander back down across the oval a couple of hundred metres to their dormitories. However, this night they waited till everyone was ready and slowly moved off in a large group, obviously protecting against prowling werewolves. I thought what a perfect chance to play a practical joke, and scare them, so I shot out the back door, barefoot; Two-Ring sprang from his slumber, thinking I was playing a game,

I silently ran down my driveway in the soft powder-like dust and was separated from the oval by a hibiscus hedge. I planned to get in front of them and jump out from behind the canteen to scare them. When I got close to them, I could hear them murmuring to each other as they slowly made their way across the oval. Because of the dust, they couldn't hear me. As I was running, Two-Ring jumped up at me, joining in the game, so I whacked him on his snout to stop him. Well, I couldn't have wished for a better result, he let out a very convincing Werewolf type howl, And the kids took off; it seemed like it was two seconds later, the dorm doors slammed shut. The next morning I had to *fess up* that it was Two-Ring and me when the students were telling their stories of how they had narrowly escaped the clutches of a real Werewolf the previous night.

On many occasions, especially when on duty nights, the students would invite me to play cards, usually a game called *"Las Kat."*(last card) The first person who finished their cards was the winner. However, the kids all cheated unashamedly, all of a sudden, after one moment of having a fist full of cards, they would be declaring *"Las Kat"*. I would order all the players to stand up, and cards would be dropping out from everywhere, *"ol kat I kam we?"* (where did those cards come from?) they would say infuriatingly, with cheeky grins on their faces. In the end, I would play their style and try and out-cheat them, sometimes not too subtly; when they challenged me for cheating, I would threaten them with grass cutting punishment; it was great fun.

From the very early days at Raval, after the students learnt my name was Andy, they started calling me *"Andy*

Mapi," do you know him? They would ask, he's a great actor, *Andy Mapi*. I had no idea who they were talking about, until we showed a film starring Audie Murphy, as soon as he appeared all the students started chanting, *Andy Mapi!!, Andy Mapi!!,* so, the famous Actor, *Andy Mapi,* was Audie Murphy!!

I had no Duke of York students in my class, they had no roads or vehicles on the Duke of Yorks, so they would be better off learning carpentry or Plumbing. But listening to the stories about the islands sitting midway between New Ireland and New Britain in Saint Georges Channel convinced me I must go and have a look. I arranged with *Matavo Bonnie,* who was from the village of Palpal on the small island of *Mioko,* to stay at his place during the next two week term holiday. We headed out in the afternoon on the Catholic Mission boat, *"David."* The small wooden boat took cargo as well as paying passengers, the trip took quite a while, and in mid-channel, the sea was quite choppy. Having brought some beer along to help with my sea legs, I had to find a place where I could, with great difficultly but modestly, pee off the stern as the wide beamed boat bobbed around like a cork in a pisspot.

On arrival at Mioko, small kids and others paddled out to us in dugout canoes to welcome us; some of the kids were toddler age and were in charge of tiny outriggers a metre long, with just a couple of inches of freeboard. They all seemed to have light brown skin and blonde hair; they were *"Island mangkis,"* or *"DOY boyz,"* and were at home in the sea as they were out of it. *Matavo* had to tell everybody who I was, they all looked at me, and when I smiled, they returned the favour with their face filling flashing grins.

Matavo had a big family, Dad, Bonnie, his mum, numerous brothers and sisters, and Rodger the dog, his name coming from them listening to two-way radio messages. *Matavo* was the oldest and so had to help his dad out with the chores around the place, while the second-born boy, *Sevit* was in charge of my entertainment. We checked out all the sights, the Queen Emma relics, the swimming pool, the railway lines, the grave in the bush at Gilgil, the two-pronged Coconut palm, the Japanese lookout tunnel, and everything else that Sevit could think of.

We paddled an outrigger canoe across to the adjacent island Maulim, where a lot more Raval students lived; we glassed for fish cooked them on the beach and washed them down with Kulau water (green coconut). At five every afternoon, I went to the Trade store at Mioko, where I had earlier that morning purchased two stubbies of SP and put them in the

The Late John Kuau and Family at Ramale Circa 1972

Kerosine fridge's freezer. By five in the afternoon, they were just cold enough; that was the only alcohol I had on this, and future trips, to the Duke of York Islands. Those balmy days went by in a haze; the other Raval students who lived on Mioko would drop around, *Negro, Rokrok,* and others, we would swim at *Nagilgil,* the beautiful white sand beach, with the blue-green water. We would glass for the brightly coloured tropical fish, then cook and eat them, and at night I would sit around with the whole family listening to the radio and telling stories.

Once again, I was at peace with the world, like I had done at Mataruru village at Bialla; I felt contented living on the island; it was such a simple existence, I was so envious of their lifestyle. It didn't worry me that I had none of the luxuries of life, a hot shower, a fridge, processed food etc. Initially, little kids would follow us around, but I became part of the furniture; they would just wave and say hello as we went by, giggling at my DOY Kuanua response.

I slept in what Bonnie called his store, a permanent building with a cement floor; I soon got used to sleeping on a mat on the hard floor. I returned many times to stay at Bonnie's place at Palpal; I travelled out on the *"David"* and the *"Raun,"* a trading boat from *"Maulim."* Then I purchased my jet boat from some missionaries, which had a Holden 179 Engine. The problem with my boat was the Starter motor was on the bottom of the engine, so immersed in the bilge's saltwater, which would rust through the starter brush springs, and then the engine wouldn't start. I started taking a spare reconditioned starter with me on my travels wrapped up in a waterproof plastic bag; I also began staying at other villages in the Duke of Yorks, such as *Kabilomo, Watara, Butlivuan,* with other students.

At *Watara,* once a big storm blew up, and as the anchorage, there was open to the elements, I decided to move into the shelter of *Mioko* harbour with just the help of a small kid as*"boskru."* I got the engine going as the little boy pulled up the anchor; the sea was very rough as I slowly headed parallel to the coast, where the sea was crashing onto the reef just thirty metres away. The boy was standing in the chain locker in the bow, with the waves crashing over him; he was having a ball, looking back at me with a massive grin on his face. He was oblivious to the fact that the boat was taking on water from the heavy seas, and then to my horror, first one cylinder stopped working from wet electrics, then another, and another. I realised I shouldn't have moved the boat into the open sea.

I was putting along on three cylinders, with just enough power to keep me off the rocks, praying I wouldn't lose another cylinder. I was getting closer and closer to the rocks and was trying to calculate if I would get to the entrance to *Maulim* harbour before I got smashed to pieces.

It was close, but finally, I passed the rocks; I gave a massive sigh of relief as I drew level with the harbour entrance near *Maulim;* I could see a little boy paddling a canoe around on the calm surface inside the harbour. I had to go past the Passage, turn ninety degrees, and come surfing into the safe water on a wave, with the wind behind me. The boat responded to the calm water, the heat from the engine dried off the wet plugs, and I was very soon at full speed skimming across the water as if nothing had happened. The boy in the front was prancing around on the bow like a mad thing. Enjoying the pace, he was waving to all his wantoks paddling around in their canoes.

Once when I was staying with Bonnie, I was invited to a Palpal wedding; I quizzed Bonnie on the protocol, not wishing to offend anyone; I told Bonnie I had nothing to give as a present, he told me not to worry, but I did. I remembered I had a large denomination bank-note, which I always carried in case of an emergency. I decided to give it to the couple in an envelope. It seemed to go down well; then all the guests were required to stand in a line and receive a bunch of customary *Buai* (betel nut). There was much consternation as the delegation neared where I was standing, a quick *kivung* (Discussion) and one guy raced off, coming back shortly with two stubbies of SP. They presented to me with the same ceremony as the *buai* to the others. To much amusement and applause from those assembled. I had not been worried about receiving the *buai*, as I had planned to give them to Bonnie.

Some years later, my boat engine eventually tossed in the towel; I had it on a trailer near the yacht club. I considered the boat not worth fixing, after a while, I received a letter from the yacht club saying if I didn't move my boat by a specific date, they would take it to the dump, which solved my problem ignored their letter and the boat disappeared.

A friend of mine *Ron Riesner* was the Headmaster of Malabunga High School; he had a boat which he left at my place and allowed me to use at any time, so I still had a way to get out to the Duke of York Islands, but he sold the boat when he went finish from Rabaul in about 1976.

I did go back to the Duke of Yorks later, even when I didn't have a boat. One time, my neighbour *Gam Pidik*, a celebrated Teacher and Artist, asked me to officiate as a judge in the string band competition at the *Duke of York Show*. I was more than happy to do this; I had a long time interest in the Duke of York style string bands. These bands had a couple of acoustic guitars and a barrage of ukuleles, which they played at lightning speed. Some of the singing was in a falsetto, years before Tiny Tim; it was fun to see the D.O.Y. boys dancing to this music. I was pleased to see the band I thought was the best and the other judges choice in the judging. At my time at Raval, we entered two string bands in the Tolai Warwagira, the Duke of York, Raval Drifters, and the Tolai style, *Brown Rice string, band*

Once Bob was on duty one weekend, he asked me if I wanted to go fishing; he had found a dinghy and some gill nets and took the D.O.Y. students out to Vudal beach to set the nets. I thought that would be good fun, so with the Gilligans, and all the Students in our truck, along with the dinghy and gill nets, we headed out to Vudal Agricultural college beach. Bob set the nets with some of the students' help, and we settled down to spend the night on the beach, eating BBQ fish and drinking a few coldies. Bob was up checking the nets through the night, every time he did, there was fish there, so the trip was considered a success.

One Saturday morning at the Rabaul market, I met up with a couple of guys I knew from *Taubar*, out Bitapaka way. They were grade 12's, schooling at Keravat National High school, and they invited me to come out to the Dance they were having the following Saturday. I headed out the next week, with half a dozen of my Raval students, who had shown a desire to attend the dance, as well. *The Keravat School Band*, which was very good, played at the dance, which was fabulous and didn't finish till midnight. After the dance, I drove my car to the other side of the playing field, and we sat around telling stories and consumed the carton of SP that I had found in my esky.

When it was time to go, the Taubar guys thought that I wasn't in a fit state to drive back to Raval, so I should sleep in one of the empty beds in the grade 12 dorm. Most of the students had gone home for the weekend, so there was plenty of space; this was fine by me, as the grade 10 guys wanted to take the Raval students with them to their Dorm. Early the next morning, I awoke to the sound of one of the teachers, *Maurice Wilson,* coming through the dorm looking for the duty students who had failed to start the water pump up.

Luckily he didn't remove the laplap covering me; my friends said it was ok anyway for me to sleep there, as they were allowed to have their friends stay with them over the weekends.

On some weeknights, I would drive into Rabaul for a drink at the Yacht club, which I had joined when I first arrived in town; many *"Chalkies,"* especially from Boisen High school, drank there. We occupied the portion of the bar that was farthest from the yachting types, who would dress in *faux naval uniforms* at times on the weekend, much to our amusement. I met *Ken Burridge* here; he was to become a good friend; Ken was an art teacher at Boisen and liked to drink a lot; he eventually went to Australia in 1984.

One Saturday morning, I came into the club to find the barman with a handful of serviettes blocking off the pie warmer cracks; I asked him what he was doing. He told me that there was a rat in there eating the pies, and he had blocked it in and turned up the warmer to the maximum heat to cook it. I decided I would drink somewhere else that day; the cooking rat's odour was not especially appealing.

The yacht club had a crest in the middle of the bar floor, and if you happened to walk on it, you had to "shout the bar," all members were aware of this, so they usually gave it a wide berth. But one night, a Kiwi guy I knew was a ship's Captain, but only ever known by his nickname, "The Coral Queen," came into the bar a bit worse for wear and staggered straight over the crest. "Shout the bar," yelled the yachtie types, offering up their empty gin and tonic glasses; C.Q. looked confused for a while, then he got it. He went to the crest, dropped his "dacks," and spun around on the Crest on his bare arse. The Committee were horrified; the Coral Queen was ejected and spent some months suspended from the club. At the bar's Chalkies end, we thought this sequence of events hilarious and got some dirty looks from the yachting types. I had already was admonished for buying a "stink boat" but was quite happy having an engine, remembering my disastrous effort at yachting at Kobuan in Bougainville.

Heading out to the Duke of York Islands, I always liked to have a bit of fun when I came to the sand spit at the end of Matupit Island; my boat was a jet I could fly over short sections of sand. The first time I did this, kids were swimming in the water there; they saw me coming, thinking I would veer off at the last minute, but I didn't. As the kids fled for high ground, I zoomed over the end of the spit; after that, they would see me coming and would scramble out of the water to higher ground where they would be jumping about and whooping with delight.

On the Victorian Football League grand final day, I was over at the Gilligans, listening on the Radio Australia network to Collingwood's footy. At the quarter time breaks, they gave the South Australian scores, and my team, the Norwood-Redlegs, were going well. After the VFL had finished, they did not provide the SA final score, so Bob and I decided to see if I could ring through to my local hotel, the *Aldgate Pump Inn*, in South Australia, to ask some of my friends about the footy score. Our School phone was a battery-powered radio phone; you had to press the button on the microphone to speak, then say *"over"* and release the button to receive. I finally got through to the Adelaide exchange, and they asked what number; I told them I was after the Aldgate Pump Inn but did not know the number, they could not understand what place I was talking about, and I had to repeat the *"Aldgate Pump Inn"* several times. As we had been on the giggle juice all afternoon, both Bob and I were in hysterics by this time as I kept repeating, *"the Pump Inn."* They finally understood, just as well as I had tears of laughter blocking my eyes by this time, they put me through to the pub, where I chatted with some of my mates and found out Norwood had won. A senior Journalist from the Adelaide Advertiser newspaper was also in the bar and did a piece on page two of the paper that week. *"How did the Redlegs go... over,"* it was Andy Fletcher from the jungles of East New Britain in PNG, talking on a battery-powered radio-phone, to his mates at the Aldgate Pump Inn. It then named all the guys I chatted too, and explained what I was doing in a bush school in PNG.

Papua New Guinea already had self-Government by this time, and on the 16th September 1975, PNG was to gain full Independence. Leading up to this, the students would say jokingly, *"are you afraid? the night of the long knives is getting closer."* I would just laugh, but a lot of Australians were packing up and moving out.

Many of them were used to an *apartheid system* and treated their workers very poorly. In clubs like the New Guinea club, you would hear these bigoted individuals abusing the bar staff using foul racist language. I would nod and wink at the barmen, telling them that these people would be gone soon, but we would still be here.

Independence came with *"Eliudia Kiapring,"* one of the National staff at Raval, ringing the school bell at midnight to welcome in a new era of Freedom from the Colonial Master that they had long anticipated. Of course, nothing much changed; life went on, as usual, many expatriates had fled to Australia, predicting doom and gloom after they had gone. But after a while, most of these people replaced by qualified PNG Nationals. PNG was now independent; I also had to move on; a National would now take my position. I went back to work at Tutt Bryant, while my post at Raval lay dormant for a year, then taken by a Philipino.

Nan organised for my students to do a whip-around and presented me with a nice Seiko watch at my farewell function; I treasured that watch for many years, as my two years at Raval were happy years.

Chapter 5

Malay-town 1976

When I started work again with Tutt Bryants, they offered me a room in their single quarters on 2/22nd street as accommodation. As these were just single rooms in a dormitory with a shared kitchen and lounge, I decided to find a quieter place. I found a lovely flat up above Hennessey's Bakery in Mango Avenue, it was right in the middle of town and had everything that I needed, it wasn't long before I found out why this lovely cheap flat was vacant. They started making the bread about 1 am, right underneath the flat, bashing the tin bread moulds about, making it difficult to sleep. However, one advantage was I could go to the bakery door at 6 am and buy a fresh warm loaf of bread for breakfast.

I only lasted a couple of weeks there, as I found another place to stay; this was a massive five-bedroom two-story house in *Ah Chee Avenue* in *Malay town*. Apart from the five large bedrooms upstairs, it had a big L shaped lounge and a bathroom. Downstairs it had another lounge, and dining room, a kitchen and another bathroom, all this for $120.00 a month. The main feature of the house was the upstairs lounge, stained glass casement windows. A significant part of the downstairs was a large warehouse, to which I did not have access. Out in the backyard was a large accommodation compound for labour lines in transit to plantations in Bougainville. Ensconced in one of these huts was an old fellow who told me he was looking after the place for *"the missus,"* so I also employed him as *"Hausboi."*

At times, I noticed Duke of York families sleeping on the shop fronts at *Ah-tam*, where the boats left for the islands, due to the boats' overloading. I thought that now I had such a large house. I could put these people up overnight until they could get another transport home. To repay the kindness the Duke of York people had shown me on my visits out there.

So I put a *"toksave"* out, and it wasn't long before DOY people would turn up, sometimes whole families, they would sleep and have *kaikai* (food) free of charge. The next day, they would wander down to *Ah-tam* to see what boats were coming in from the Islands and organise their passage. Next door lived Gam Pidik, a Duke of York big man, and his family, which included *Eliuda Laen*, his son, a student at *George Brown High School* (GBHS). The school was a United Church school, named after the first missionary who lived on the Islands at Port Hunter. Laen was, like his father, a very talented artist; he would draw magnificent freehand ink on paper, traditional drawings.

It wasn't long before some people asked if they could stay more than just an overnight stay; *Michael Luiana* was a day-student, doing his PETT course at Malaguna Technical College, and had nowhere to live. His cousin *Michael Kalaman,* was a student at *Malabunga high school*; he would also visit, then stay the weekends. Many others remained for a few weeks and then went back home. My doss-house at least prevented people from sleeping outside on the *Ah-tam* shopfronts.

The two Michaels became good friends of mine over the years; Michael Kalaman, when he finished at Malabunga, went to Keravat National high; I was then working as a lecturer at Vudal, living in a forestry house next to the Police Station at Keravat. Michael would come down to the house with his friends to cook up a feast after classes; when he graduated from Keravat NHS, he got a job with *LAES,* just up the road, to work as an agronomist with DPI. His house was not far from one of my favourite haunts, the *North Coast Sports Club,* and on many occasions, I would bludge a bed there when the Keravat river flooded, and the bridge went under, and I couldn't get back to the College.

After graduating from Maltech, Michael Luiana got a job as a barman with one of the hotels in *Bougainville* and became a rugby league star; I saw him again when he came to Rabaul with one of *Jim King's* Rugby League teams.

I would show films in the upstairs lounge for my house guests and a few of the neighbours. Sometimes during holidays, students from GBHS would stop over, coming back to school, and they asked me if I could come out to the school to show films. I told them I would if the Principal approved; the students asked the Principal, who then sent me a letter asking if I would donate my time, projector, and a film, to show at the school, one night a week. I had to make sure the films were suitable for a *"Christian School,"* which was hard, there are only so many times you can show *Bambi!* I agreed to this and then had to source action films with no swearing, no sex, and were not too gory. George Brown was a co-educational school, and the staff felt they needed to shield the female students from all this sin.

The films were shown in the chapel; They removed the large cross off the end wall and used the wall as the screen. The picture screenings were very popular with both the students and staff, at the school, I managed to find enough suitable films for them. One night, however, I had a film which was an action film, basically one long car chase across America; in the end, the car pursued by police ploughs into two bulldozers parked across the highway. A small part in the film where a young lady rides out of the desert, naked, on a motorcycle. As soon as I saw the bike coming, I put my hand over the lens to censor this part of the film. The students, especially the boys, were hooting and *ssssh'ing*, not happy at missing the best part. I could not see the film on my hand as it was out of focus, so I listened for the sound-track to cue me when this unsuitable scene was over. I eventually heard the motorbike start up again and ride off, so I removed my hand from the censorship position. Unfortunately, I was a little premature, as up on the screen appeared the backside of a naked lady riding a motorcycle into the sunset, whistles and hoots of appreciation from the boys greeted this tiny glimpse of the scene. *"Stop the film,"* shouted the Principal as he jumped up from his chair. *I don't think we will need any more films "lights on, all the girls file out please, now the boys,... sorry Mr Fletcher."* So that was the end of the movies for George Brown. The students were all waiting outside to find out how the film finished; they were not very happy the film nights had come to an end.

At work, Tutt Bryant were agents for Komatsu earthmoving equipment, and I went out to service or repair machines wherever they were working. One time I went to Bougainville to do some work on a device on the other side of the *yellow river*. I spent the whole day working on the Public works dozer and finished up late in the afternoon. I drove a works Landcruiser and headed back towards Kieta and the hotel where I was staying. When I got to the Panguna turnoff on a whim, I decided to head up to the mine to have a look and see if I could get a free meal. When I arrived at the Karrewong Haus mess, I marched in like I owned the place, straight into the Mess Supervisor's arms. He was the same one from my time. Sprung, I thought, bugger, *"Back again, eh, I knew you couldn't stay away,"* he said. *Phew,* I decided not to correct him; as I loaded my plate up from the buffet, Bougainville Copper was still providing excellent meals for their staff, and this night, one interloper as well!!

I was sent to Namatanai in New Ireland to service the Komatsu's working on extending the road in the *"Las Kona"* (last corner) area. This time I was allocated a driver by works, despite my request to drive myself. We headed off for the road head, with the driver driving like a maniac on the narrow *karanas* (crushed coral) coast-road that passed through many beach-side villages. I tried to enjoy the beautiful scenery; I tried to tell the driver to slow down, which he ignored, and count the chooks and pigs that we cleaned up on the white knuckle ride through the villages. I was petrified a small kid would run onto the road and get hit, and both the driver and I would be hacked to death by the angry villagers as *payback*.

We eventually arrived at the end of the road, and I could start servicing the dozers; on the return journey, I took the keys from the driver and told him I was going to drive. He only agreed after I threatened to report his driving to his boss, though he sulked back to Namatanai. I had a leisurely drive, stopping at places of interest to take photos, and smiled and waved at the villagers. Hoping they had forgotten how we had driven at a maniacal speed through their villages, cleaning up chooks and pigs just a few hours earlier.

I stayed overnight at Namatanai Guest-house, where I met the owner *Mike Kanin*, who also had the Post Office and other town businesses. Mike told me the club was showing a movie that night, so I wandered down to check it out and have a few drinks. The Namatanai club was right on the beach and was a charming place to drink and watch a movie. Mike was an ex-teacher; he had taught at *Kabatirai* on the Duke of York's; he was a pleasant guy with a great sense of humour; we had an entertaining chat about life on DOY.

I had borrowed the movie *"The Adventures of Barry Mackenzie"* from the New Guinea club to show at home, so I invited a few people around, one of whom was *Ken Burridge*. Burridge turned up with Mataungan Stalwart *John Kaputin*, and his Ex-pat girlfriend; the movie was funny, basically portraying Aussies as drunken yobbo's. John was not impressed; he considered the film to be approving of the Australian lifestyle, so he turned his back on the movie and went to sleep on the lounge in protest. Both Ken and John's girlfriend tried to get him to watch, but he refused.

I still attended village 626 dances and became a member of the *Nangananga sports club*, the only white member. On a Saturday, I went to *Turagunan* to visit *"Big Bel,"* with a cold carton of SP in my esky and spent a pleasant afternoon consuming it. In the beautiful pink light of dusk, I went with his kids with their *"pornok"* to shoot some birds. Watching them miss their quarry many times, I asked for a go. I brought a flying fox flapping down with my first shot, *"wow, wan moa,"* said the kids. But there was no way that I would show that I had fluked it the first time. As the night air got darker, fire-flies started flashing in-sync on the bushes, so we squashed some on our forehead and headed back to *"Big Bel's"* house with twinkling lights on our heads.

Big Bel produced a 40 oz Bacardi and one large bottle of coke, so the two of us started mixing and drinking as the beer had finished. After some time, I can vaguely remember pouring the remainder of the coke into the Bacardi bottle, and fuzzily I can remember waking up during the night, with rain pelting down, wanting to vomit. The bush material house was on stilts about six foot off the ground and had five fence posts of descending heights stuck in the mud as a ladder.

This ladder was challenging to negotiate when sober but was impossible when drunk; as I staggered outside to vomit, I missed the second post and fell flat on my face in the mud. I couldn't get back up the ladder, so I just konked out in the mud. The next morning I awoke to find I was sharing my *"bedroom"* with some pigs, who were snuffling about my person, *"moh, moh, moh,"* looking for something edible for their breakfast. (This house is still there and is known locally as *"The sleeping with pig's house."*) As I had finished off the Bacardi by myself, I headed back to Rabaul for a shower, suffering from alcohol poisoning.

Three days later, still feeling unwell, I drove out to the out-patients at Nonga Hospital, but the nurses chased me away when they found out my malady was alcohol-induced. This episode was a wake-up call for me; never again would I drink myself into oblivion. While I was still in control, I would go and sleep. To this day, I have not been able to stand the smell of *Bacardi* and have never drunk it again; it also took me a couple of years before I could drink Coca Cola again.

Most of the tracks that made do as roads throughout the Gazelle were volcanic pumice, which was great to drive on. Even when they turned to torrents during rain, the base was stable, and the car would not get bogged. The thing to watch for was where the water ran across the road and carved out a deep trench, some big enough to swallow a car like mine, though it was very seldom that I ever got stuck. After heavy rain, the tracks that did have washouts, the local villagers repaired. They had to have the roads open to get their Produce to market, their kids to school, and themselves to work.

Kulau Lodge was a Restaurant and accommodation Units, a few miles out on the North Coast Road, at *Kabakada village*. I quite often would go out for the $2,00 Sunday buffet luncheon. *Brian Connelly* owned Kulau at this time; he was also part of the film swapping group. The head barman was a Milne bay guy called *Marcel,* a friend of mine; getting near closing time, *Marcel* and the other staff would hide beers under the bar behind the clean glasses. Brian would lock up the fridge at closing time, after checking that I didn't want another drink, and head back to town; the staff would then bring out the hidden beer and sit around drinking in the *haus-win*

When paying for my lunch one day, Brian informed me that the Buffet price had gone up from $2.00 to $3.00; I complained that my wages hadn't gone up, to which he replied with a grin, "*mine have.*" It wasn't long before Brian sold out to *Peter Leggett*, but *Kulau Lodge* continued to be a favourite spot for Sunday lunch for me. I told Brian years later, after I got to know him well, about what had gone on after he had locked up the fridge and left. He told me he always suspected something, as I was always still hanging around when he left, but he was never sure what was going on.

When working for Tutts, the boss told us that the new PNG currency, the Kina, was being introduced, and we would have a choice of being paid in Australian dollars or *PNG Kina*. I opted for what everyone was calling the "*funny money*," the *Kina*, as I had already decided my future lay in PNG, most other expatriate staff chose Australian Dollars. I had the last laugh as the Kina was not a floating currency. It was-set to be worth more than the U.S. Dollar. A few years later, when I travelled to the USA for holidays, one Kina would buy U. S. $1.50.

Now that PNG was an independent country, I had to get an Australian passport and a work permit. People who had lived in PNG for more than eight years at Independence could apply for Citizenship, but as I had only been there for five years, I was not eligible. I am sure I would have if I were; it did not worry me that I would have had to renounce my Australian Citizenship, as I felt far more at home in PNG than I ever had in Australia. By the time I got my eight years up, I had worked on three-year expatriate contracts for the PNG Department of Primary Industries, Education and Training branch. If I took out Citizenship then, I would have gone onto local wages. So

I decided that while I was working for the Government and still being offered contracts, I would stick with my Australian Citizenship. As it was twenty-three years later that I finally finished up with DPI Education and Training, circumstances had changed, and I was then offered contracts with the Education Department

It was greed that stopped me from taking out PNG Citizenship; I did take out PNG Residency but did not have to relinquish my Australian Citizenship. I justified this selfish stance by acknowledging that I always got paid more than my local counterparts. But I did share my money around. I don't think I ever refused a request from friends who were struggling with the financial burden of educating their children. Over the thirty-six years I lived in PNG; I must have financially helped thousands of kids get an education. This use of my money that I otherwise would have pissed up against a wall gave me a tremendous buzz, especially students who otherwise would not have got an education.

Just down the road from my house was *Chang's Restaurant*, their chicken curry was a favourite of mine, and I would get a take away at times when I was too lazy to cook. Their other food was also first class, and I looked forward to the times we would get a group together to go there for a meal.

I was sent out around the New Guinea Islands on-field jobs to service and repair Komatsu's but sometimes also on other jobs. One time I had to go to a Plantation on North Buka to repair a Volvo-Penta engine on their boat. I flew across to Buka Passage by a regular flight, then by *"Bougair"* charter in a single-engine Cessna, to the plantation. When I arrived at Buka passage, the Pilot looked worried at my heavy tool-box. He agreed to take it but told me he could not take off from the plantation strip on the return flight with that load, so I would have to make other arrangements for the return trip.

As we were belting down the runway at Buka Passage on take-off, with the plane vibrating and rattling, my door flew open; he told me it did that sometimes and could I hold it closed, which I had to for the whole white knuckle flight. As we arrived at the plantation, with me still grimly clutching the door handle, I could see what he was talking about with the short strip. From the air, the airstrip looked only a couple of hundred metres long, and at both ends was a stand of very tall coconut palms. We dived down on approach, clipping the palm fronds as we went past, then swooped down to the ground; immediately, the pilot stood on the brakes as a wall of coconut palms came rushing towards us. He managed to stop but reminded me again he would not be able to come and pick me up.

The Plantation people were there to meet me and took me down to where the boat mooring. I was left to my own devices with the *boskru* (boat crew) of the boat, Robert, to help me. I very quickly found the engine had a cracked cylinder head and removed it. At *Belo kaikai* (lunch) I was called up to the plantation house, then went back down to the boat to finish removing the head. Robert had some mechanical experience and was a great help. After inspecting the head, I explained that I would have to take it back to get it welded in Rabaul. Luckily, I would not go back by plane as the cylinder head's extra weight now made air travel impossible.

The plantation people told me I would travel by sea in the Plantations' *Mon*; a big long sea-going canoe carved out of one large tree. The next morning after spending a pleasant night drinking a few coldies with the plantation people, updating them on what had happened in Rabaul since Independence. I headed off early with Robert as *boskru*, operating the 40 hp motor; I had a comfortable seat right in the middle; it even had cushions and an esky which held my lunch, some snacks, and a few beers. We were to head down to a plantation where we would overnight, then motor into Buka passage the next morning. That trip in the *Mon* was memorable; the sea was as smooth as glass as we headed down through the reefs of the offshore islands. Robert had his trolling line out with a piece of colourful *trukai rice* bag as a lure, and we would have to slow down now and then as he pulled in another large fish. I had some snacks for morning tea, then checking where the yardarm would be on the *Mon*, if it indeed had one. I calculated that the sun would most definitely have been over it. Therefore it must be time for a nice cold SP. I sprawled out on my very comfortable seat, at peace with this beautiful world, thoroughly relaxed, keeping my neck well lubricated but taking in everything around me. On the shore, I glimpsed splashes of colour from birds high in the virgin rainforest canopy.

Out west on the horizon were thunderstorms with lightning flashes; the balmy atmosphere was still and loaded with humidity, giving the scene a surreal look, like an old painting and arriving at dusk at the plantation we were to sleep overnight and escorted through the reef to the jetty. I was still on a bit of a high after the fabulous boat trip. But I was whisked away to the plantation house to dress for dinner. The people on this plantation were also happy to have someone to talk to, as they didn't get many visitors. They had prepared a meal but apologised that they had to use *kaukau chips*, (sweet potato chips) as they had run out of potatoes. I thought they were magnificent, as I had never tried sweet potato chips before, we sat up till the early hours, telling stories and making inroads into their alcohol stash.

The next morning after very little sleep, it was time to head off for Buka Passage, and though I felt fragile at first, due to the amount of alcohol I had consumed the previous day, I soon got my sea legs. I was starting to feel like an old salt after spending all of the last day at sea as we motored into Buka Passage around lunch-time, in plenty of time for my scheduled flight. I bade farewell to Robert, who was keen to get the fish he had caught up to the market and hitched a ride out to the airport with my heavy cargo. It wasn't long before I was on the flight back to Rabaul, day-dreaming about the beautiful canoe trip down the west coast of Buka. I unsuccessfully tried to recognise the terrain from the plane window as we flew out over the west coast, heading home.

I told the boss I would be happy to take the head back and fit it after repairs. But they told me Robert had watched how I had removed it and was going to replace it by himself. I can't blame them; they had calculated how much my trip had cost them, with the cost of beer, food and transport, and decided it would be far cheaper for them to do it themselves.

After working at Tutts for some time in 1976, Boroko Motors asked me to work for them as the Workshop Manager, and I moved away from Tutts for the last time. Working for Boroko Motors as the Workshop Manager meant that I would not be working with tools; I would allocate jobs and organise the workshop. From this time on, I would never again work as a mechanic; I would hold more senior positions.

Many Expatriates and Nationals drank at the *"Chalkies"* end of the bar at the Rabaul yacht club; *Bob Cogger* was one. Bob was a Senior Lecturer at the Vudal Agricultural College out past Keravat, and his wife Sue was the Mess Supervisor. I had got to know Bob through the *"Chalkie's bar,"* and he told me one day that the college was looking for a Mechanics Instructor, and would I be interested. After assuring him I would be, he organised an interview with the Deputy Principal. After a few weeks, I was signed up to work for the Department of Primary Industries Education and Training Branch as a Mechanical Instructor. I gave notice at Boroko motors and moved out of the big house in Ah Chee Avenue.

Chapter 6

Keravat 1977/1980

I t was late January 1977 when I first started work at Vudal Agricultural College. Unfortunately, there was no accommodation for me at the Campus at that time. So I was asked if I would mind living in a big three-bedroom forestry residence next to the Keravat Police Station. The house had been vacant for some time after a previous tenant had died in the place. The house being-haunted, new tenants only lasted one night there; they would be scared off by the ghost. I did not believe in ghosts, which, coupled with my drinking a large quantity of alcohol before sleeping, meant I slept like a baby, the first night, and every other night after that. Ghosts can only harm you if you believe in them. The house was a Forestry house and built from PNG hardwoods; it had three bedrooms and a lounge/dining area in the main home. A large front deck looked out over the road and the Keravat river flood plain. Out the back was a large breezeway that separated the kitchen and bathroom from the main house. The house set on posts about a metre from the ground.

Not long after I moved in, *Michael Kalaman* wandered in with a big grin on his face; he had been chosen to attend Grade eleven and twelve at Keravat National high school, which backed onto my house. Michael had not known about my move to Vudal, so he was delighted when he spotted me at my new home, which bordered the school's path down to the shops at Keravat. He and his friends would drop in regularly after that, cook up a big pot of rice, tin fish, or ox and palm bully beef when they felt hungry.

I had a fifteen-minute drive to work every day but was on the other side of the Keravat river to the College, and as there was only a low-level bridge spanning the river. Many times after heavy tropical rain, the bridge would be a metre underwater, and I would be cut off from work. My Boss in the Rural Engineering Section at Vudal was Mick O'Callaghan; he was a lovely old bloke getting near retirement age and was understanding about the river. He just loved working with the big Russian lathe that was in the machine shop.

My Holden station wagon was getting a bit worn out, so I sold it and bought a Datsun 1000 Ute from *Ted Whitaker;* Ted had a guest house in Rabaul and had a dodgy reputation. I initially was a bit wary of buying a car from him, but he had the car in his name on the Registration papers, and the car seemed ok mechanically. Also, the price was right, so I took a chance. I got to know Ted pretty well after that; I did hear stories from other people about how Ted had ripped them off, though I never had any problem with him myself. Ted had worked for The Corrective Services. He had been in charge of the *Wewak Kalabus* but had ended up in his prison after fiddling the books.

Ted had won a lottery and brought PNG's favourite singer of the time, *Slim Dusty*, to Port Moresby to play at a Rugby League ground. He planned to make a killing with ticket sales for the Concert. Things looked very promising on the day, as the Concert was well advertised, thousands of excited Slim Dusty fans massed outside the Ground in anticipation. Only a few had paid the gate to get in by the time the music started. The hordes outside, afraid of missing out on seeing Slim and his band, swarmed the fence, knocked it down, getting in for free. Ted made a massive loss on his venture as a music promoter and lost his entire lottery winnings while paying off Slim and his entourage.

After work at Vudal, I would head up to the North Coast Sports Club in my little Datsun ute for a drink, it was too far to go into Rabaul on a week-night, so I now had a new drinking hole.

It was not long before I was on the Committee and met *David Loh,* the Club Manager; David was the Lowlands Agricultural Experimental Station Manager. David, was a Horticulturalist, had a favourite saying, *"You can lead a horse to water, but you can't lead a whore to culture."* The Clubhouse, the nine-hole golf course, and cricket oval all stood on LAES land. Most of the Ex-pats in Keravat and the National staff of LAES, Vudal, and Keravat High School were members. The club held a film night on Thursday nights, some Saturday night dances, and a BBQ on Sundays, but mostly it was where everyone went for a drink after work. David had been doing the film night, but it wasn't long before I took that over; as I was still heavily into the film swapping scene, I also started showing films at my house.

Initially, I showed a few films in my lounge, but with many people peering through the windows, I decided to build a screen on my front lawn and screen the movies from my front deck. The word soon got out about the free movies at my house, and most of the population of Keravat, and even as far afield as Napapar, would turn up with mats to sit on the lawn and watch the movies. Some Nights I would get a bit carried away and spend more time at the club than I had intended while people were waiting back at Keravat to watch a film.

On these occasions, the Police paddy-wagon would drive up to the club, where I was still drinking, turn around in the car park and head back, just to remind me. The other drinkers would freak out when the Police turned up, as on the first three days of the week, the club was supposed to close at 8 pm, so quite often, we would be drinking illegally. I would then have to take the hint and head off back to Keravat, where I would find people walking around to the village, disappointed that there was no movie. As soon as they saw my car, the call would call out *"piksa, piksa, piksa"* and turn around and run after the car.

The students from the National High School behind my house were allowed to watch the films, but only after 9 pm when their compulsory night study was over. Right on 9 pm, thirty to forty students would come running, like a herd of buffalo, thundering down through the Kamarere block at full gallop, the house would start vibrating. They would come bursting through the back door, through the house, and jostle for the best positions on the front deck. Out of breath but laughing at the slow coaches who had to sit at the back. Some nights would get washed out by rain, but I would show the film the next night, some nights I had no movie to watch, and some nights the films were not popular like a Romance. But everyone was ok with that, as the film showings were free, and if anyone found the film boring, they would wander off. The families at the Police station next door kept the front lawn raked and the screen maintained. The films became a popular pastime for the Keravat residents until I moved up to Vudal later when a house became available.

We held open dances at the club, which were attended mainly by Plantation labourers from the surrounding Plantations; the club members would not participate in them as the dances were too rough. We persevered with them for quite some time as they were very profitable because we held them on the labourer's pay-days. It was usually David, Sue Cogger on the till, and me, who turned up to run them. When the bar was seething, and everyone was drinking Bacardi and coke in plastic cups, one night, I went to help David, and John, the barman, to serve the drinks. I said to Sue and David that we better change the Bacardi bottle; as I had noticed it had been empty for about half an hour, we all burst out laughing as the punters had been getting drunker and drunker, falling about the bar, on only the coke and ice.

Once a year at the club held a *"Rum Cup"* this was a golf game that was open to everybody, but the rules were unusual. Each group of four golfers went out to play. With a waiter with a rum bottle After every hole, each player had the option of reducing their score by downing a shot of rum, for each nip you had a golf shot removed, if you had a double bogey on the hole, by downing two shots of rum you would end up with a par.

Of course, the worse you were at golf, the more rum you had to consume to stay in the game; this proved to be my downfall, being a very average golfer. I made it to the last green very much under the weather but tied in the golf with my nearest rival. We sat on the green downing shots of rum, the lead changing hands several times; my opponent had the advantage over me as he was a good golfer and had only drunk a couple of rums up to the last hole. I started to turn green from the large number of rum shots I'd had; feeling quite ill, I crawled over to the bunker and threw it all up. I immediately was disqualified; you had to keep the rum down; I think that was the closest I ever came to winning a game of golf.

I went onto the Committee of the NCSC in my first year. Then I was voted onto every Committee after that until I was transferred to Kavieng nine years later. When I was first on the Committee, the club's male toilet facilities consisted of one sit down toilet bowl; on big nights, this was a problem until we got a urinal installed. I went to use the toilet bowl one night, just for a leak and found a mouse swimming around in the bowl. I came back to the bar. David said, did you see Johnny Mousemuller in the toilet. I said I thought it looked more like Loraine Crapp; this resulted in a laughing fit; I think both of us had consumed too much of the giggle juice. Having a house adjacent to Keravat National High School was convenient for Ken Burridge, who had been transferred from Boisen high, to teach at Keravat; he could wander down during his off periods for a snack and a drink. He still lived in Rabaul and always had to have a cold six-pack to sustain himself on the one hour journey to and from town.

I would buy my beer in a twenty-four bottle carton of stubbies, and as Ken also spent a lot of time drinking after school and during free periods at my breezeway, I soon started accumulating many cartons of empties. At the time, a carton of empties fetched one Kina, ten Toea, so I stored them in my kitchen to cash in at a later date. Soon the kitchen got so full there was only a narrow passage-way through the empty cartons, from the door around to the stove and sink. I eventually called in the contractor who purchased the bottles and loaded them on his truck, and I received a small windfall.

I usually drove into Rabaul every Saturday morning to buy some fresh veggies and fruit from the market; my favourites were the large banana-shaped *"Rabaul Mangoes,"* the sweet, acid-less pineapples, small Pacific banana, and Guavas. After the market, I would head to the Kaivuna motel *"Haus Win"* for lunch and the afternoon session. Ken, David, Brian from Kulau, and Richard, the Travelodge Manager, plus others would meet up there on Saturday afternoons and Friday nights. Richard, always dressed immaculately in high waisted jeans, with a kalakala shirt, and had glasses with lenses made from coke bottles' bottoms. Richard also had his mother's knowledge to fall back on; I think their farewell must have been a long one. His homespun wisdom would include things like *"My mother warned me about people like you,"* and My Mother told me to *"Never trust anyone who had a monobrow"* sheesh! All my dear ole mum warned me was to wipe the toilet seat. The Saturday arvo session was always good fun, but I had to get to Andersons on Malaguna road for my freezer and grocery shopping before they closed at six, then head home. Every time I headed out from Keravat for my Saturday shopping trip, there would be some of the high school students waiting for a ride into town as well; they would all jump in the back of the Datsun. One time as we're coming down the steep winding Burmah road, my rear wheel rolled past, then bang was down on the brake drum. The students retrieved the wheel, which had rolled off into the *kakao,* and by taking one wheel nut from the other wheels, we were mobile again. Most of the students who came with me would catch a PMV back out to Keravat, but sometimes they would be waiting at Anderson's for a ride home.

I had contracted malaria many times since I had been in PNG; however, in 1979, I came down with a very virulent Cerebral malaria strain, which nearly finished me off. A lot of people had come down with this strain. It had killed quite a few people, including the Westpac Bank Manager, who had managed my overdraft for me without any fees, for quite a few years. One morning, I woke to feel a bout of malaria coming on, I took some chloroquine tablets and stayed in bed, but the fever got worse. The hot spells where I went and stood under a cold shower, then the cold shivering where I had to pile blankets on. At 11 am I went into a coma and was like this until about 5 pm. When I recovered slightly and back to the hot and cold cycle, the next day was the hot and cold cycle, then on the third day precisely at 11 am went into a coma again, 48 hours after the first one. It happened three times, and as I was home alone at the time, after the third time, I drove myself through Toma out to Kokopo to the Catholic Mission hospital, *Vunapope.*

They admitted me there, and after I told them what had been happening, the doctor confirmed I had Cerebral Malaria; they gave me pure Quinine. I was still pretty sick but when the 48-hour deadline came around for the fourth 11 am coma, it passed without a problem, so I knew they had broken its back. I stayed in the hospital for a few days and visited by a young female German volunteer Nutritionist; she was a *"stout"* lady with legs like a billiard table. Her English had a thick German accent, so when she came to see me, she affirmed, *"Ya Mister Fleisher you are anaemik ya, und ve must built up the ret korpuskles, vis da spinach und red meat ya."* I was so crook I had lost my appetite, but I was too scared not to agree with her. She came back after my meal and *tsk, tsk'ed* my plate, which was still half full, *"The ret korpuskles, Mister Fleisher,"* she admonished. I was back on track after a couple of weeks, as my Red Corpuscles had improved, and a side effect of having gone through this drama was that I never got malaria ever again. I was immune, suffering from cerebral malaria, obviously was either going to kill me or cure me and luckily for me, it chose the latter.

Mike Hunt, the Livestock senior lecturer at Vudal, was a mad keen cricketer, and once he found out that I had played cricket in Australia, he was on to me to play for the Keravat team. I was not so keen when it came to chasing a cricket ball around a paddock in the scorching tropical sun, or sitting in the cool shade, downing ice-cold beers; there was no contest. But Mike was persistent; he would come and get me out of the various bars, saying the team needed me, and he would drag me kicking and screaming into the hot mid-day sun. On cricket days, when I did not want to play, I eventually found a safe-haven, that Mike never checked, the *Iapidik club* at Malaguna no. 3 at the bottom of the *Burmah road*. I became a regular there and even joined the darts team, which would play against other village clubs, such as the *Gordon dry boys club* and the *Malmaluan club*. I would drive my car around the front onto the beach, so not visible from the road. Mike would quiz me on Monday, trying to find out where I had been hiding.

On the days I did play cricket, I suppose I did enjoy it if it was not too hot, and when we played at our home ground, the NCSC, I could sneak off and have a quick drink at the bar. When we were short of players, Mike would ask me to bring a few Papuan students from the High School, as they were naturally good cricketers. One day at Queens Park, Mike and I made an opening stand of around 200 runs; this story took up the whole back page of the Monday Post Courier. Even though I now lived out at Keravat, I still roamed far and wide, looking for 626 dances and discovering new village clubs. The old *Kapa* (corrugated iron) Nangananga Sports club had been replaced by a new one called

smiling happy villagers Rabaul ENBP>

Nason Memorial club. A Saturday, after spending all day at the Iapidik club, I was told that there was a dance at the *Nason club.* So I headed up to *Nangananga* with some of my friends from *Malaguna 3.* The dance was a good one, but as I was full before I arrived, and starting to konk out by about midnight, so I snuck out to my car and went to sleep.

My mates wondering what had happened to me, came looking for me and dragged me back inside, despite my protestations that I wanted to sleep. The first chance I got, I was out to the car again and fast asleep once more, but once again, they took me back inside, so as I made my escape next time, I looked for somewhere else to sleep. I moved silently through the moonlit village, looking for a friend's house, but became a little disorientated and found myself at the *Haus Lotu* (church). I could still vaguely hear the music from the club as I made my way to the pulpit, where at last I could get some uninterrupted sleep in peace on the floor. Sometime during the night, I pulled the laplap from the pulpit as a chill descended on the night air.

The next thing I remember, I could hear my name called out from far off in the distance; I was not asleep but not yet awake, as I felt somebody shaking me, the voices got louder, and through my sleep haze, I realised somebody was talking to me. *"Andy, Andy, Andy, mipela laik lotu ia"* (Andy, we want to have our church service.) I was wide awake. There was a group of scowling village women, in their *Sunday best Bilas*, looking down at me, a dishevelled drunkard, asleep on their pulpit. *"Sori, Sori, mi stap we?"* (sorry, where am I) I said feebly, embarrassed at my predicament; I replaced the *laplap* and stood up, my head spinning. Wishing I could have had a few hours more sleep, but deciding on the spot that I shouldn't ask the good folk of *Nangananga* if they minded if I had a bit more sleep.

As I wandered unsteadily outside, all the blonde headed little kids clutching their *Gud Nius Bibles* sought refuge behind their mother's *laplaps*. They were staring wide-eyed as I left their church. Maybe the sermon that day was about the evils of the Demon Drink. With a real live drunkard to put up as an example. My friends from Malaguna had looked for me at the end of the Dance, but having no luck, gave-up, and got a ride back into town with someone else. It was quite a while before I was game to show my face at the Nason Club, but recounting the story to some of my Nangananga friends at a later date had them in stitches; they thought it was a great joke, but I couldn't forget the looks on those ladies faces.

Another club I went to was *The Seawall club*, on the Kokopo road, about midway between Rabaul and Kokopo. They served an excellent lamb flab stew there, and after a drinking session, there was nothing like a greasy lamb flap stew in your stomach. They also had a jukebox, which had my current favourite song, *"It's all over now baby blue,"* my air guitar rendition was infamous at the Seawall.

As I got to know Brian, Richard, and David better, we started going out on picnics to the many beaches around the Gazelle. My favourite spots were *Reivan,* and surrounding beaches, *Vunairima*, and even out to some of the inland rivers. We would usually take enough food to feed a small army, as most beaches belonged to local villages, and it was an acceptable policy to provide for everyone who came down to the beach.

We would arrive before mid-day as we had to listen *to Kasey Kasem's* top *100 hit parade,* David had a glass that held about a litre, and he would make himself a few drinks, slosh them down, and after a few of these would konk out on the beach. Because of this habit, he got the nickname of *"Great Land Basking,"* to go with his other nickname, *"The Keravat Carrot,"* because of his red hair. Richard would bring his hibachi, which he would be hunched over for hours waving a fan at it, trying to get the charcoal burning. He would eventually emerge myopically with his coke bottle glasses smeared in smoke and grease, with some perfectly cooked marinated chicken, or some such. His job done, he would then join the party.

I would bring a big BBQ plate I made up in the workshop, and half a dozen of my counselling student volunteers, to help find firewood, light the fire, and cook all the food. Allowing me to join the party right from the start, Brian would entertain the crowds with a pump, pumping up his enormous belly and then doing fake vomit. For the BBQ, we would bring lamb flaps, instead of oil, a few kilos of Anderson's sausages, chicken wings, and thighs, and lots of onions to fry, many loaves of bread, salads and side dishes, tomato sauce, lolly water for the help, and the village kids. The picnic would get into full swing when David would come back to life, sit up, and pour himself a more modest drink, music supplied by either a cassette player in one of the cars or by a boom box. Sometimes some of the students would go glassing on the reef and bring back some fresh reef fish to add to the BBQ meat; I don't think anyone ever went hungry at any of our picnics.

When we would turn up at our chosen picnic destination, the village kids would come rushing down to the beach, with big grins on their faces, and immediately go searching for firewood, knowing they were going to have a full stomach that day. Some times our picnics would extend into the night; if we had food and drink left, on these occasions, we lit a bonfire, and eventually, we would head back home late at night.

At the College, staff allocated students for their counselling groups to help students out with any problems they may have in or out of the classroom. Most National Lecturers would have the students from their area. As we had students and staff from over PNG, this was pretty easy to allocate, but my being an Ex-pat was a little harder. I declared I was a local, so my counselling group was made up of New Guinea Island students.

One of the new Tolai students came to me to the first day he arrived at the college one year, his name was *Herman Valvalu*, he told me he was from *Ramale, Kokopo*, and told me when he was a small boy when I first started coming to his village, and he was one of the kids that would catch my money. These were the times when I would be approaching the village in my car; I would stop down the road and get all the silver coins I had; at the ready, the small kids would know what was coming when I turned up, so would come running. As I drove into the village, the kids would surround my car, and I would throw the handfuls of coins into the air, and the kids would dive on them. Herman was one of those kids; he laughed at the memories as he was 19 years old.

One of the girls who came over from the Police compound to rake the grass on my lawn and keep the movie area clean was a Morobe girl named *Mosingo;* she was aged 18 and worked as a domestic for one of the ex-pat teachers at the high school. She was the daughter of *Senior constable Niauru* who was a nice guy. I noticed she would look strongly at me while she was working, late one night; there was a knock on the door; it was *Mosingo*, who wanted to come inside. These late-night visits continued for quite a while and then abruptly stopped.

I did not know what had happened. I had not seen her coming over to clean-up or attend the movies. I forgot about it, then some months later, some of the Morobe students at college started calling me *Tambu*, which in Pidgin means *in-law*, and I thought they had found out about *Mosingo's* visits but just laughed it off. One day, I was drinking at the club with one of the other Morobe policemen when he told me Mosingo had given birth to a baby girl; I said to him that it was nice, but he then said the baby was mine, how he knew that. He said the child's face was the same as mine; I then asked whether the baby had a *moustache* because I did, to which he said no, so I told him that proves it, I'm not the father. With all the whispers, and the students calling me *Tambu*, I was the last person in Keravat to find out that Mosingo had been pregnant and had a baby girl.

I received a letter from Welfare telling me I had to attend a hearing in town. I went to the hearing, where I saw Mosingo for the first time for a while, and an old lady who turned out to be Mosingo's mother, and in a crib, a very light-skinned baby, already named *Esther*. Fortunately, the two girls from Welfare were friends of mine, so I felt I didn't have everyone ganging up on me; it appeared to everybody there that there was no doubt that I was the father of Esther. However, I still was not sure. Esther's father in the birthing book at the *Keravat clinic* was Andy Fletcher. The Welfare court between Mosingo's mother and me started, though Mosingo was 19 years old when the baby was born and should have spoken for herself.

The first thing the girls asked me was, did I want to bring up the baby, to which I replied no, they then asked Mosingo's mother what she wanted, and she said twenty *kina* a fortnight, which was a fair bit in 1980. I would have been happy with that, though, but the Welfare girls jumped in, telling the mother that that was far too much; Andy couldn't afford that, we'll make it ten *kina*, to which I just nodded. I think the Welfare girls had instantly disliked Mosingo's mother and went in to bat for me. So that was that I organised a direct debit into Mosingo's account and didn't see Esther again until 27 years later.

A few months later, *Niaru* transferred to Kainantu in the highlands; a couple of years later, I received a letter with Esther's photos aged about three, Niaru moved again, and I went to the *Fisheries college in Kavieng,* and we lost touch altogether. Some years later, my support money which was still paid, was stopped by the bank; I could not find out why, so when one of the Morobe students at Fisheries College was going on leave, I asked him to find out what was going on. When he returned, he told me Esther, who was then at high school, had died of Malaria. That explained why my payment stopped. I accepted that this was the truth, until many years later, in 2007, when Esther was 27 years old, she contacted me, wanting to make contact, so we met up in Kavieng. I asked her about the stopping of the money; this was because Mosingo married a guy who wanted to bring up Esther himself, and at the same time, Esther did have very bad malaria but survived.

To show films, I had access to the Vudal film and the NCSC film, which I would swap with many schools, clubs and institutions; I would have three or four movies in my house at any one time. One of the biggest dealers in films was a school teacher *Bob Godsell*; he even had a picture theatre at the *Vunairoto primary school*, on the turn off down to *Kulau Lodge* on the North Coast Road. Bob was a friendly guy; he had a wonderful sense of humour and loved everything about movies. One day Bob told me the latest blockbuster film Jaws was being shown on Saturday matinee at *Kadat theatre* at *Kokopo* and did I want to go with him to watch it. The place was packed, there was a lot of small kids in the row in front of us, and when the scene came up, where the shark came right out of the water lunging at the guy in the boat, the kids in front of us climbed right over the back of their seats into our laps, they were so scared, we thought it was so funny, pushing them back into their seats.

Bob Gilligan was still the plumbing instructor at Raval when the NCSC Committee approved new septic and pipes for the club; I suggested that we get Bob and his crew to do the job, as they would be far cheaper than a qualified plumbing contractor. One afternoon the Raval truck turned up to my house with about 15 students and all their rations and tools. I had two spare bedrooms, so it wasn't a problem, they had also brought their food, but I helped out topping it up with some extra kaikai and kumu (greens) from the market. They stayed for a few weeks until they finished the job; it was a pleasure having some interaction again with Raval. I went on holiday to visit my Mum over Christmas and was asked by my brother to join him and some of his mates on a *Great Barrier Reef fishing trip*. I had not seen *Sean* and *Sally*, my Brother's kids since they were little; Krys, my Sister in Law, always thought I was a drunk, she had been telling her kids, they had an alcoholic Uncle living in PNG. So when she picked them up from high-school to meet me at the Mount Gravatt footy club, I got my legs tangled in the bar stool as I went to stand up to meet them and fell flat on my face. I could see Krys nodding knowingly!!! I was only on my second drink.

A house was now ready for me on Campus at Vudal, so I moved.

Chapter 7

Vudal 1980/85

T he house I moved into at Vudal was on the far side of the College; it was on metre high stilts, had two bedrooms, and floor to ceiling louvres which made it cool; I was happy with it. Being on Campus now meant that I would have to take my turn at being a duty teacher, the College had both male and female students, so naturally, there were more problems. Most of the students were older than I was used to at Raval, and the majority came from the highlands region.

I soon got used to living out at Vudal; it was a beautiful setting with the college buildings spread out over a large area, with gardens, lawns and giant rain trees well established. My Section, Rural Technology, was a big complex down the other side of the oval, including Building Construction, with Carlos, a Filipino.

I still frequented the North Coast Sports Club on week-nights and went to the *Yachtie, Kaivuna,* and *Iapidik club,* on the weekends, as well as searching out the 626 dances wherever they might be. My Datsun had the floor rust out, so I decided to replace it with a new second-hand car from the upcoming Works Auction after patching it.

I had observed the locals did not like Automatic cars because if the battery went flat, you could not push start them. Push starting of cars being quite common in PNG. When the acid had dissolved the lead plates inside the batteries, no charging or even replacing the acid would re-invigorate the battery. It did not prevent people from trying to get more out of a dead battery.

The Auction held in the works yard had many Mazda 323 station wagons, land cruisers, and a VIP Mazda 929. I checked out the 323's before the Auction; however, I noticed that all were manual gearboxes, so be popular with the locals. The VIP Mazda was an Automatic; this would be better to bid for, as none of the locals would be interested when they found it was Automatic. The 929 was the first car up for Auction; as many people crowded around, I said in a loud voice, *"Oh no it's automatic,"* the locals straight away lost interest and went off to check the stick-shift 323's. One other ex-pat and I started bidding, and when it got up to Kina 920.00, he said to me, *"Do you want this car Andy?"* I told him yes, I would try and outbid him. He decided to withdraw and let me have it, he later bid for and got one of the 323's, and I got my Ex VIP Mazda, with Air conditioning, carpet, and Cassette player, for a very reasonable K920.00.

One Sunday morning, after a heavy night out, I drove across to Kokopo and out past Vunapope to where you could go down onto the beach. Some stacked logs placed there, waiting for a log ship to come and take them, so I climbed up on one of them and enjoyed the tranquil surroundings. Suddenly, along the road came the *Malabunga High School* truck. with students singing in the back, they turned down onto the beach, and a grade nine class jumped out for their annual class picnic. The girls all moved off up the coast with the Lady teacher. The boys produced a volley-ball and started playing in the water, near where I was. Four of the boys came over to where I was sitting on the logs; I recognised one of the boys from *Ralalar*, one of my stomping grounds. He identified himself as *David Dude* (Pron. Dooday), we started telling stories, including my infamous Nangananga church episode, which David and his friends had heard about, and thought was hilarious.

The girls and the teacher were about a hundred yards away up the beach. Most of the boys were throwing the volley-ball around in the water. When a scream came from a boy as he disappeared under the water. I looked up as he screamed and just saw him go under the water. I, like everyone else, thought he was playing and waited for him to resurface. After a short while, I yelled out to one of the boys to see where he was; he said he was sleeping on the bottom, so I told them to get him up quickly. The Tolai lady teacher came sprinting up the beach, dived in and retrieved him; they quickly got him into the truck and took him to Vunapope hospital five minutes up the road.

About an hour later, the truck returned with everyone on the back howling in grief; the hospital couldn't revive him. I later found out the boy was from Morobe Province; he had a medical condition that caused him to have Epileptic fits, which happened in the water. The boy was to be School Captain the following year, and his drowning was a big shock to his family, class-mates, and the whole school. There was some suggestion from the family that there could have been foul play, so one of the Malabunga teachers, *Joan Duigu,* married to a Vudal lecturer, and lived just across from me, came to see me. I told her the full story of what had happened. He was not near any other kids; there was no foul play involved; he screamed and went underwater. How the lady teacher was there in a flash, got him up, and to the hospital as quickly as was possible, obviously it was only his medical condition that was to blame.

David Dude was to become a good friend from then on, he would come with some of his friends from School for weekends, instead of going home, and later when he had finished school, he continued to be a good mate.

After some time avoiding the *Nason club*, I again went there for a dance; I was pretty sure I was not likely to meet up with any of the Ladies who had chased me out from the church. I was pretty sure none of them would frequent a drinking club, so I felt safe. The dance was a good one, good music, good friendly crowd, and I made sure I didn't drink too much and needed to find somewhere to sleep. It was here that I met *Peter Wakanga,* I already knew his older brother who worked at *Taubman's Paints,* but I had never met Peter before. Peter was a typical Tolai, he was twenty years old, but still very shy, he lived just down from the club at *Nangananga.* he seemed impressed with my Kuanua, which was probably at its peak at that time, and laughed at all my jokes. Peter was after a job at Vudal, so I told him I could help him out, and he became part of the Vudal community for a time. He joined the *North Coast Sports Club* and was a gun on the eight ball-table He did not drink alcohol, but his friendly natural personality shone through after he overcame his shyness.

Peter returned to *Nangananga* at the request of his family, I would see him at future dances, and he remained a good friend. I was shocked to hear not long after; he had passed away from *malaria*; I am always so sad when young people pass away, especially a special friend; Rest in Peace Peter.

Brian, and David, who owned some juke-boxes in Rabaul, asked me to look out for music and buy records when I was on holidays in the West Indies. I got some crop-over records in Barbados, some Rita Marley and other Reggae music, and on my way home picked up *"Ebony and Ivory,"* by *Paul McCartney* and *Stevie Wonder,* which had just been released in the U.S. that day.

Brian put the records in his jukebox at the Kaivuna straight away, and a day or two later, I was having a drink with a Salesman from down south. He told me he had heard *"Ebony and Ivory"* on the radio in Sydney, and he couldn't wait for it to-be-released in Australia. I strolled over to the jukebox and put it on; he couldn't believe that this song wasn't yet released in Australia and was on the remote PNG jukebox. Yes, said Brian, with a huge grin; we had it brought in by courier from the U.S.

At one of our picnics on the beach at George Brown High School, I decided to go for a swim late in the day. Many Duke of York schoolkids were still on the beach, as we had already fed them, so I moved up the coast a bit where no one was swimming. The sea was fairly rough, but here it seemed smoother, and it wasn't long before I was heading out to sea in a violent rip. Having had a few drinks, I forgot all I knew about swimming sideways out of a Rip and tried to swim straight into the beach.

A grade nine Duke of York boy on the beach saw what was happening and swum out to me, telling me to swim parallel to the shore, then once out of the rip to swim in with him to the beach. I was beginning to struggle before the boy reached me and felt a bit of a fool, as I did know what to do. The DOY boy said he had seen me out at his village and that his name was *Robin ToVatup*. He had watched me going to where the rip was and knew it was dangerous, as some of his classmates had been in trouble there earlier in the afternoon, so he had followed me along the beach just in case I got in trouble, lucky he did.

I told him to tell his parents that I would pay his entire grade ten school fees for the next year for his assistance in saving me from drowning. Later, his father visited me to see if this was true; I told him what his son had done, so it was true. After Robin finished his grade-ten, I was surprised to see he won a position at Vudal and came and did his Agricultural course there. After graduation, he was taken on by the College as an instructor in livestock, looking after the chickens. So from a chance and lucky encounter for me, Robin ended up being a colleague at Vudal. I don't think I ever met a happier PNG person than Robin *ToVatup*; he always had an enormous grin on his face. I was lucky that I could repay his quick thinking by backing him in his chosen career.

Oscar Natera was Principal when I first arrived at Vudal; we then had *Joe Maza, Yawal Mazewin, and Jacob Sawanga. Jacob* had been *Senior Lecturer* in Livestock before he was appointed *Principal*, his wife *Bing* was also a lecturer at the College. I had by this time risen from being an *Instructor* to a *Lecturer*, then the *Senior Lecturer Rural Engineering*. I got on very well with Jacob and would ask my advice on problems he had, and then his younger brother Aquila came to the college as a student. Aquila was in my counselling group; he was a good student; his prospects were very bright; he had a chance to be the Dux of his year.

He came to see me one day about withdrawing from College; I asked him why, and he told me his brother was on his back all the time, and it made him very unhappy. I told him not to do anything until I had a talk to Jacob about him. Jacob said that just because Aquila was his brother, he wasn't to get any special treatment from him, why he was so hard on him; he didn't want any other student to say that Aquila was getting preferential treatment. I told Jacob I thought he wasn't giving Aquila special treatment but was unfairly targeting him.

I suggested that Jacob should leave any disciplinary action for Aquila to me. And for Jacob to distance himself from him at the College. But to treat him like his brother when he came over to his house. I then had a talk to Aquila and asked him to let me know if Jacob gave him a hard time; I told him of the arrangement, and urged him to stay on, which he did, Jacob stuck to his word and didn't hassle him, and Aquila graduated with flying colours.

A few years later, I got a phone call from Aquila, thanking me for persuading him to stay on at Vudal, as he now had an excellent job with Consort shipping in Lae. Many more years later, when I was shifting from Kavieng to Port Moresby, I rang Aquila, who was General Manager of Consort, about my lost container, which was somewhere in his yard. He went out and personally found it; he then rang me, apologised profusely, and made sure it was on the next possible ship to Port Moresby.

Jacob let me handle most of the discipline matters regarding the students, as the students trusted me to be fair and balanced and listen to all the evidence before taking any action. When we had to terminate four students for some quite serious crimes, the whole student body went on strike; they wanted the four reinstated and sat on the Basketball court until they got what they wanted. I went and sat down with them, listened to their views, answered all their questions, and then told them that I didn't think they were aware of what the four students had done. After I had finished telling them, I asked them what they thought the College should do; they were unanimous, the students expelled. So they dispersed back to their classes, and the four students concerned expelled.

During the High School Careers week, I would visit the High Schools in the New Guinea Islands region to give Careers in Agriculture talks. We had visual aids such as pamphlets and videotapes; we would take it in turns at going to the different provinces, one year when I was doing New Ireland and Manus. I went to New Ireland and gave talks at Namatanai, Mangaii, Mongop, Utu, and Madina, high Schools. The night before I was to fly to Manus, Cyril, the Lorengau Hotel manager, rang me in Kavieng. He told me that the Hotel would not be able to pick me up at Momote Airport, as Prince Charles was arriving about the same time as me, and he was very busy with all his guests.

As we flew into Momote, I could see hundreds of traditional Manus dancers and official dignitaries assembled, waiting for Prince Charles, Royal Air-force aircraft. As our Air Niugini flight came to a halt, I was the first one out the door; I was in seat 1A, I stopped at the top of the gangway and gave a rendition of the air stirring Royal wave. Immediately the Manus *garamut drums* started beating, and the dances started up, "*hey, hey,*" then someone said, "*that's not him,*" and the drumming stopped. Someone behind me in the plane said, "*get a move on up front,*" and my moment in the sun at being a Celebrity evaporated.

I waited around with everybody else for the arrival of *Prince Charles*; when he eventually arrived. He rushed off to *Lombrum*. It was the cue for everyone else to jump in their cars and take off, and in no time at all, the car park was emptying. In desperation, I asked the guy from Shorncliffe, the *kolta People* (bitumen laying) who were in the province sealing the roads, if I could get a lift with him. He said he only had space on the back of the ute with the drums of Kolta, it was either that or walk, so I jumped on. As I arrived at the hotel, Prince Charles had boarded a Patrol Boat at *Lombrum Naval Base* and was slowly steaming into *Seaddler harbour,* escorted by hundreds of sea-going Manus Canoes. I dumped my bag in my room and walked down to the town beach to watch as the Prince transferred to one of the canoes. To be escorted into the beach, and carried up the beach, to be met by *Nahau Rooney.* There were massed dance groups from every village in the Province, the *garamut's* (native drums) were deafening, and all the dancers wore traditional bilas. No sign of any bra's here; this was the real thing, it was very stirring, spine-tingling stuff, and Prince Charles seemed impressed. Something I will never forget, and at the time felt so proud for the Manus People; I'm sure Prince Charles has never forgotten that welcome also.

When I got back to the hotel, I met Cyril, who was in a panic, as he had Journalists, PNG Government Premiers, and other Politicians staying at the hotel. And the dining room and reception had recently been destroyed by fire. I went and freshened up in my room, removing my *kolta*-soiled trousers, and returned to the big Haus-Win, (Pergola), which now housed the bar, restaurant, and reception. I spent the night chatting to Cyril and some English Photographers. The Premier of West New Britain also joined us and some other provincial politicians; by the time I headed off to bed, they were getting very drunk. The next morning as I left my room for breakfast, one of the provincial politicians was fast asleep in the flower bed in front of my room, covered in vomit. I asked one of the Security to help him to his room before a photographer spotted him. After the provincial authorities completed all the official activities, I eventually met my careers week.

At Vudal, we employed an old West New Britain guy called Matalombo; he was the tea-maker, cleaner, general dogsbody, and the morning flag flyer. Matalombo only had one arm, so he had to pull the rope of the flag down with his arm, hold the rope with his teeth, then get another grip on the rope, and pull it down with his arm again, until he had the flag fully raised. After fifteen years of service, Matalombo was granted six months furlough leave, as long as he trained one of the Labourers to take over his position temporarily.

He picked a guy out of the general labour line and spent a couple of days training him up, making the tea, flying the flag, washing the cups, etc. Matalombo departed, and as we assembled for a cup of tea before classes the next morning. As the new handyman raised the flag the same way Matalombo had shown him, we watched in disbelief, holding the rope in his teeth and using only one arm to raise the flag. I took pity on him and went out and showed him how to do it, using both his hands.

Being head of the Department, I had to attend many meetings, workshops, etc., with colleagues from the other two Agricultural Colleges, *Popondetta*, *Mount Hagen*, and the Headquarter staff. I participated in a Curriculum review meeting at Popondetta. I learned a good friend of mine from my Bougainville days, *Peni Amos*, was the golf pro at the golf club, which was not that far away, so I got a lift with a staff member going into town after school and told him when he dropped me off, that I would get a ride home with someone at the club.

Peni was not at the club, and the barman didn't know if he would be coming in or not, so I settled down to have a few cold ones. Before I knew it, the bar was closed, everyone had gone home, and I faced about a five-kilometre walk back to the college by road. According to my calculations, though, the road went around in a great big loop back to the College, but as the crow flies, it would be no more than a kilometre if I took a short cut. I headed off down a well-worn track in the general direction of the college, patting myself on the back for being so smart; I would be back at the College in no time; this track probably went right there. There was a full moon, so I had no problem seeing where I was going, but to my disappointment, the trail petered out at a sago swamp; I looked around both ways, trying to find another track heading through the swamp, but to no avail. It looked like I would have to risk the *"Papuan Black"* Taipan snakes and *crocodiles* and run straight through the middle of the swamp. I immediately was up to my knees in the thick black oozing stinking mud, falling frequently, and being jabbed by the sharp needles on the sago fronds, in places where I slid over the sludge and water. After what seemed like hours, I emerged, like *"the creature from the black lagoon,"* covered from head to toe in vile stinking mud. The sago barbs ripped my clothes, which had also cut and scratched me all over, drawing blood. I also had lost my thongs in the mire. Though at least my calculations were right, I had emerged at the boundary to the college. The students looked amused at my appearance as I walked past the dorms to my host's house. One of them called out, *"Mister, yu kam we?"* (Mister, where have you been)I said *"Golf klab,")* (Golf Club) he replied, *"Nogat rot ia,"* (there is no track), to which I said, *"I gat"* (yes, there is) they all burst out laughing *"rait man, brukim Saksak".* (Right man, made his track through the sago swamp)

My hosts were shocked at my appearance and my story, but it was nothing a good shower, some Dettol, and a box of Band-Aids didn't fix. The next morning as I walked to the staff room, the students heading to class all smiled when they greeted me; no doubt I was the butt of all their jokes that morning. The staff, though, couldn't believe I actually got through the swamp, and descriptions from my hosts at what I had looked like after my ordeal, certainly did not need any embellishments.

At the end of that eventful meeting, I was asked by one of the Livestock Lecturers if I would take a cage full of breeding pigeons with me on the aircraft, back to Vudal, for the Senior lecturer Livestock. I was flying to Port Moresby that Friday, then had a connecting flight on to *Rabaul* the same day.

However, things didn't go to plan; waiting in the departure lounge in Moresby, the PA system announced, *"Passemumble, PX mumble Rabmumble, pleasmumble mumble, counter,"* our flight was cancelled.

We recovered our luggage, which for me included the pigeons, and were sent to hotels around town and told to return to the airport the next morning. They sent me to the Boroko hotel. But I now had a problem, as I'd be staying overnight, the pigeons would get hungry and thirsty, I couldn't do anything about the hungry, but I could give them a drink. I found a reasonably clean ashtray, filled it up with water, and tried to slip it in the cage without letting the birds out, but to my dismay, the pigeons saw their chance at freedom and took it, the whole lot of them got out. They flapped around the room, settling on the curtains; I grabbed a chair to stand on, and with a lot of swearing and grabbing handfuls of feathers, one by one, I eventually got all of them back in their cage.

The room was in a mess with feathers everywhere. As I departed the room the next morning, the cleaning lady was standing outside, waiting to get in to service the room. She gave me a pleasant smile as I fled to the reception, hoping the courtesy bus would be there waiting for me. No such luck, I had to wait in the reception area for the bus; a short time later, the cleaning lady came to the reception, whispered to the girl behind the counter, and they both turned and glared at me. I responded by smiling innocently back at them, the cleaner turned and went back to her job of cleaning up my just vacated room, and I wondered what they thought had gone on in there during the night.

I arrived back at the Airport to find that we were to fly to Rabaul via Lae, so we were again on the move. When we tried to land at Lae, the town airstrip fogged in, we tried a couple of times, but each time the pilot had to abort. So he turned around and flew out to *Nadzab*, a large international airport out in the Markham valley. Which had been an Independence present from Australia to

PNG, was now abandoned, but we landed there anyway. They told us we had to stay here and wait for another aircraft, as this plane had been ordered back to Port Moresby, with our luggage on board. We wandered over to the large departure and arrivals hall to find it locked up. So we sat there out in the hot sun with no food or water, waiting for another plane to come and pick us up.

Eventually, an Air Niugini van arrived from Lae, with bottles of water and scotch finger biscuits for us. As lunch-time approached, four of us decided we would walk out to the road and catch a *PMV* (Passenger Motor Vehicle) into *Lae* to buy some lunch. In *Lae,* we dropped into the *Melo bottom bar* (Melanesian Hotel) near the town airport. And had a couple of coldies and bought some chicken wings and chips for lunch. We were worried that our plane might turn up at Nadzab while we were in town, so we didn't linger. We caught a *PMV* back out to *Nadzab* to find everyone was still waiting quite impatiently. At the airport, we sat around, walked out to the road and back again, inspected the runway for foreign objects, and got crankier and crankier; we thought they had forgotten us.

Then just at dusk, a plane arrived from Port Moresby to take us on to the *Lakunai strip* in Rabaul; as we got airborne, the Pilot informed us. As it had surprisingly got dark, we couldn't land in Rabaul, as they had no landing lights, we would be diverting directly to Kavieng.

I spent that night at the Kavieng Hotel, and the next morning we flew across to Rabaul, where I inquired about my luggage. I found out that my bags, including the Pigeons, had arrived the previous day. They had rung up Vudal to come and pick the Pigeons up, so they were already at their new home. My other luggage was still there at the terminal waiting for me. I had taken three days to get from Popondetta to Rabaul, but my luggage only took two, known in *PNG* as a *"TANGFU."*

In the final two years at Vudal, I moved into a United Nations house, that though new, had been empty for a year. I convinced Jacob that the house was wasted just sitting there, and even though it didn't belong to us, we might as well use it. Having a high set house with a big entertaining area underneath, I decided to hold a house warming party. On a Saturday, I invited Staff, my counselling group, and many friends from town and Keravat for the occasion. I had a half sheep on a spit and a BBQ and lots of refreshments, including non-alcoholic drinks for the students. Tony Wong from the Keravat Post Office turned up with a big bowl of his famous raw fish, and other guests contributed food and drink. The party went all day, and well into the night, and was a great success, though I think there were sore heads in the morning.

Some people reading this narrative to the point may get the impression that I was an alcoholic; many, nay most, of my adventures so far have involved alcohol. I want to point out that PNG revolved around clubs and hotels. The sporting events, social events, such as dances, everything involved a certain amount of alcohol, and if you were a wowser, you would have had a very dull time in PNG.

However, while initially drinking almost every day when I first arrived in Rabaul, I progressively cut back my intake until living in Kavieng. I only drank at the club on the weekends, and following that, when I moved to Port

Moresby, only on Sundays. So I was sort of like a *"reverse alcoholic,"* from drinking every day early on to being an occasional drinker as I got older and wiser.

Tony Wong was of mixed race and ran the Keravat Post office with his wife Alu; they were also members of the NCSC, Alu was an excellent golfer, and Tony was the big brother of famous singer John Wong. One night when we had a Ball at the club in Keravat, I was at the bar with *Sue Cogger* and *David Loh,* when Tony and Alu made their grand entrance, fashionably late, all dressed up to the nines. Sue said she mistook them for an expatriate couple at first, to which David quipped (with apologies to Arthur Caldwell) *"Two Wong's will never make a white,"* which cracked Sue up.

Though I had already passed thirty, I coached an Aussie rules team comprising students from Vudal and Keravat National High School and student from Vunairima Seminary, Samson Lowa. A couple of teachers from *George Brown High School* were involved, including *Api Maha,* from the famous Aussie rules Maha family of Port Moresby. *Samson Lowa* later had a very successful career with the United Church, ending up as the Moderator. Our team was a perfect one; we had many young and some very skilled older players. I played a quarter here and there if we were short of players. But when the temperature on the field was over 40 degrees Celsius and the humidity was 100%, I usually left it up to the younger guys.

I had a visit from a good mate of mine from South Australia, *Aivairs Strazdins,* who was very fit and still ran Marathons; he wanted to play in our team in a game we had at *Vunairima* oval at *George Brown High School.* I think he had never played in that sort of heat before; he was exhausted before the end of the game. It was also pretty bad for me, as I had to umpire because the official umpire hadn't turned up. This team broke up prematurely, as there was a scandal involving an Expatriate Priest at the High School, and all the high school players had to withdraw.

Some twenty years later, Samson was the United Church Moderator and was on an official Church visit to New Ireland; I met him at Kavieng Airport on his arrival. All the United church school kids lined the road with flowers. Samson arrived and was greeted with much pomp, ceremony, and fresh flower Leis, by the local dignitaries. As he emerged from the arrival hall, he spotted me. I was the Air Niugini Port Manager at the time; I shook hands with him and said, *"Do you remember me, Samson,"* to which he replied, *"I certainly do; how are you, Andy."*

He was whisked away by the local Church dignitaries, a little embarrassed that their leader knew me, the long term President of that *"Haus of Sin,"* the Kavieng Club. Samson looked back, smiled and waved; I'm sure he was dying to catch up and reminisce about those early days when he was a footy playing student.

One day, *Denius,* a George Brown High School student from Watara, Duke of York islands, turned up on my doorstep, telling me the school had expelled him for having sex with a Teacher's daughter. He was too scared to go home and tell his family, so I contacted the school to see if they would reconsider his expulsion. They wouldn't, and the other high schools were also adamant they did not want him. So I enrolled him at *Raval Vocational* for the rest of the year and then sent him home at Christmas to see what his family wanted him to do the following year.

In January, he returned from DOY with a message from his father requesting that I look after him until he had finished school. I enrolled him again at Raval. He stayed as a boarder until I was transferred to the Fisheries College in Kavieng. I then organised his transfer to Lemakot *Vocational Centre*, a Catholic Mission Vocational school in New Ireland.

One Sunday morning, I was driving out past Kokopo; I came around a corner onto a single-vehicle accident; a 3-ton PMV truck had overturned, killing two young boys. The rest of the passengers were sitting on the side of the road in a state of shock. I stopped and asked those sitting if they were alright, but they just stared blankly back at me; another car came along and stopped; I asked them to go to Vunapope and get them to send the Ambulance and inform the Police. I checked the dead boys. One had his hand sliced off but otherwise looked ok, but had passed away as had another boy. I waited for the ambulance and the police to arrive and then left; it was very upsetting to see two young lives lost for no reason at all.

One Christmas, Burns Philp Ship's Captain, *"Coral Queen,"* invited some of us to attend the Burns Philp Christmas party on Mioko Island in the Duke of York Islands. I accepted the invitation. We took off from *Rabaul* in one of the big coastal barges, all the B P's staff sat up the back and threw out fishing lines. We were up near the wheelhouse to give the skipper constructive advice on how to steer his ship.

About half-way across, the skipper said watch this, and swung the wheel to full lock and did a complete 360-degree turn, much to the chagrin of the BP's staff, who got all their fishing lines tangled. We moored off *Togilgil* at *Mioko*; as the team were still trying to untangle their lines, I headed off around the track to Palpal to invite Bonny and his family around for our BBQ. It was great to catch up with so many of my friends at Palpal who had looked after me on my earlier visits here.

I got an invitation from Ted Whitaker, now known as *"Donpos,"* which means *"man, who smokes a lot,"* by the people of *Maso Village Pomio*. To come down to *Pomio*, to officiate as a judge at the *Pomio Show*. I boarded a coastal copra boat with Richard and David on a scheduled voyage to the Pomio Villages. The trip was an overnight one, and by morning we were approaching *Palmalmal*. Later in the day, we eventually arrived at *Maso*. Ted greeted us and showed us around his three-storied bush material mansion, including his house, guest house, bakery, and Post

Tavurvur Volcano in Rabaul Harbour after the 1994 Eruption

Office. I had to judge the participants in the various sections of the Show; I helped judge the Traditional dance with some village elders from the surrounding villages. We were especially tough on anybody who showed any western type attire, such as wristwatches, bra's, or shorts.

The show was a great success, and some traditional dances that were dormant for many years were on display. The evenings I spent in the snooker hall of Ted's Palace, where he also served cold SP. Some days later, we caught a third level Airline from the grass Maso strip to fly back to Rabaul via Palmalmal. I was sitting up front next to the Pilot and when we circled Palmalmal on approach for landing. A warning light on the twin-engine Cessna showed the front wheel had not locked in. The Pilot tried to wind the wheel down by hand, but to no avail, we had to head straight for Rabaul without landing at Palmalmal. Richard and David, who were sitting up the back, were signalling me, enquiring what was wrong. I told them to pray we wouldn't crash. When we got to Rabaul, the Pilot had briefed me on the crash procedure; I moved all the passengers to the plane's rear. Then I took up a position in the seat behind the Pilot, ready to kick out the emergency exit window if we crashed. The Pilot landed softly on the two back wheels, with the warning light still showing the front wheel still wasn't locked in. Aided by all the aircraft's weight down the back, it ran down the runway with the front wheel in the air until the speed slowed enough for the front wheel to gently come down on the tarmac. The nose-wheel did not buckle, as it turned out the warning light was faulty, not the wheel lock.

At Vudal Agricultural College, most of our students were from PNG. However, we did have students from overseas, the majority of which came from the *Solomon Islands*. One Christmas, I decided to visit the *"Solomons"* for my holiday; I had to fly to Bougainville on *Air Niugini* and then catch a *Bougair* twin-engine Cessna through to *Guadalcanal*, the Capitol of the Solomon Islands. As it was an international flight, we had to have a meal served. I wondered how this was going to happen as the only crew was the Pilot. I found out after a while; the Captain announced there were sandwiches and cold drinks in the esky behind his seat. Could the passengers come up one at a time and help themselves.

As we came in for a landing, I could see the war wreckage on Red beach just near the airport; there was very heavy fighting during World War Two. We landed, as usual, my bag was last to come out of the hold, so I was last in line for Customs and Immigration. I was standing up the back of the arrivals hall daydreaming when suddenly two guys in Quarantine uniform rushed up to me with big grins on their faces, *"Andy, Andy, come with us."* It was two of my ex Solomon students from Vudal Agricultural College. I went with them through Quarantine, much to the other passengers' disgust, for a super quick visa. They were so excited to see me and gave me V.I.P. treatment. I then had to sit down and update them on how Vudal was and how all the staff were. We chatted until all the passengers were through Customs. They then gave me a ride into town in the Government vehicle. We made arrangements to meet up at the *"G"* Club (Guadalcanal Club) the next Saturday night; this club, like the New Guinea club and the Kavieng club, was an old Colonial Club. It at one stage during World War Two hosted *General Macarthur* it had seen better times.

Honiara was a sleepy backwater; the Prison gates were left open during the day, inmates could wander around town as long as they returned before they locked the gates at 6 pm.

I spent a couple of relaxing weeks in Honiara, then flew out to *Auki* on *Malaita Island*; these people bear a remarkable resemblance to the *Tolai* and Duke of York people. Though I found their language is quite different, I tried speaking Kuanua to them.

From my earliest times visiting Ramale, I always enjoyed singing as we roamed around the Gazelle's bush tracks in my car. Not far from Ramale was the *Catholic Girls School Kabaleo*. There was a song about this place we sang. I have forgotten much of it, but it went something like this, *"all meri sikul lo Kabaleo, kam trening lo Vunavavar, o grass I wet, sori mi no save, ol blupela sikirt."* (Girls from Kabaleo with blond hair trained at Vunavavar and had blue skirts.) We would sing this with gusto as we drove through the school; great fun!

Jacob called me into his office one day to tell me ex Vudal Students *Mesulam Ave,* and *Melchior Ware*, who were now Principal, and Deputy, at the *National Fisheries College in Kavieng.* Requested I be transferred to Kavieng for a year, to replace the *Marine Engineering Lecturer,* who was on a one year course in Japan. Mesulam and Melchior were previously my students, so I knew them well. As the transfer was for one year only, I accepted. I liked Kavieng; it was a beautiful place. Jacob organised a farewell party for me at the Principal's residence, and I loaded much of my cargo into my new second-hand car, a *Mazda 929 Station-Wagon.*

I had to get a transfer for *Danius* from *Raval* and organise passage on a barge from Rabaul to Kavieng; I also took my billiard table and my traditionally carved tropical Walnut hardwood bar. Danius and I travelled on the barge with the car and cargo for a magical overnight trip to Kavieng.

Chapter 8

Kavieng 1985/94

The overnight barge trip from *Rabaul* had us disembarking at the small Market wharf in Kavieng at around 10 am; Melchior and Mesulam were there to welcome us. After they off-loaded my cargo, I drove down the *Boluminski Highway* for the five-minute drive to the Fisheries College. I was allocated a high set Government house, with an entertainment area underneath; it had previously been the Principal's house. A previous tenant had modified the house, constructing a balcony along one side. One of the three bedrooms made way to enlarge the lounge room. The house was on the highway, but there was quite a distance from the road to the house, and I had only a one minute walk to my office in the morning. The next day I drove one hour down the sealed highway to *Lemakot Catholic Mission* to enrol *Danius* as a boarder in their *Vocational Training Centre*.

My section, Marine Engineering, was on the waterfront on the other side of the town opposite the hospital; it consisted of a big machine shop, a slipway, a pier, and various other smaller buildings. The students went backwards and forwards in our bus or truck between the college and the waterfront. We slipped our boats and private ones to give the students practical work knowledge in boatbuilding and Engineering.

A few weeks after I arrived in Kavieng, *David Loh* came over from Rabaul for a long weekend. We decided to drive down the *Boluminski Highway* to *Namatanai* and stay in *Rasese Village,* where I had friends. The *Karanas road* (crushed coral) surface was quite good, so we had a leisurely drive down the very scenic highway that followed the coast all the way. We stopped to take photos and chat with the locals and stopped at Palm hill to swim in the ice-cold creek that appeared from the base of the limestone cliffs on the other side of the road. Near *Pinikidu,* we dropped in at a Plantation to see the newly married, newly appointed *Plantation Manager* and ex Vudal student *Jackson Lali.* We eventually arrived at Rasese at dusk. We cooked up a big BBQ with the meat and chicken we brought with us from Kavieng and sat around drinking and chatting till late. The next morning we drove further down the road to *"Las Kona"* (Last Corner) as far as the road went, or at least as far as we could go in a two-wheel-drive vehicle. We came across a fast-flowing river with boulders that finally stopped us in our tracks. We drove up to *Sir Julius Chan's* house at *Huris,* but only a couple of his children were home. So we went down to *Huris beach* and checked out his treetop fishing lodge overhanging the water. We then went back to stay at the *Namatanai* hotel, which Mick Gallon owned; we had a good chat with Mick over dinner and drinks and took our time driving back to Kavieng the next day.

Not long after arriving in Kavieng, I was home alone one night; *Danius* was at *lemakot,* as he only came home on the weekends. I was woken about 2 am by the sound of glass breaking under my house. I got out of bed and went to the kitchen window and could see the fluoro tube under the house had been turned in its socket; someone was trying to break into my car. I thought it was probably some of the local village lads who had been drinking and wanted to go for a joy ride, and now that I had disturbed them, they would run away.

I turned on some extra security lights, giving them plenty of time to move away, and went down to the car to remove the rotor button to disable the vehicle. I had to fiddle with the Fluoro tube to get it to light again and saw that my car's door was open and a rear quarter window broken. I lifted the bonnet to remove the rotor, and as I bent over the mudguard, I felt a bush knife pressed hard against my throat. Three *raskols* (criminals) confronted me; I didn't know these guys were hard-core criminals. They were in prison for murder, rape, and other serious crimes and had escaped from the *Kalabus* (Prison)!

They had escaped continuously from the high-security *Bomana Prison* in Port Moresby, so they were transferred to Kavieng because of Kavieng's record of no escapes. Nobody escaped from Kavieng because all the inmates served short sentences for minor crimes, like drunk and disorderly.

Earlier that day, they gave them three bush knives, and under the supervision of a warder, had been sent to the Prison Commanders house to clean up the garden. They immediately threatened the warder with the bush knives, jumped over the three-foot-high fence, and ran away. They hid out until it was dark and then tried to steal cars all around town but had been disturbed on each occasion. By the time they had walked out to *Fiscol*, it was late at night, and they were desperate to get a car; that's why they held me up when I came down, instead of running away.

They tied me up and told me they were going to rob the Westpac bank the next morning, and I was to be the hostage. They went up and ransacked my house, changing their prison clothes for my jeans and shirts. Not having eaten all day, they got stuck into the food in my fridge and started drinking my beer and a full 40 oz. Brandy. They bundled me in the back seat of my car, bound, gagged and blindfolded me, and drove back into town. Though I was blindfolded, I could tell where we were going; they drove out past the airport and onto a dirt track to wait for daylight. They then decided that this track looked too well worn, and people would start using it as it got light. So drove out again, just near the airport we encountered a Police car, out looking for them, they quickly took the blindfold and gag off me, and as we drove slowly past, the Police hardly looked at us. I don't know what the Police thought I was doing driving around at 4 am, but they didn't stop and check us out. The *Raskols* blindfolded and Gagged me again, we drove out past *Fiscol*, and *Utu High school* and turned up a more remote track near *Panapai Village*.

As daylight approached, I could hear them talking as they were swigging down my brandy. There was not much petrol in my car, so they decided two of them would take the car into town to steal some petrol, while one would stay and guard me. In the early morning dawn, two of them drove off into town; they were pretty drunk from drinking my Brandy. People were starting to go about their business, and as they drove past *Elcom*, they tried to grab a lady who was on her way to work and drag her into the car; she, fortunately, fought them off. They also knocked down and ran over an older man walking on the road. As it was my car, police received reports that Andy Fletcher had gone berserk, trying to pull ladies into his vehicle, and was running over people. So they drove out to my house to find out what was going on. When they got there, they found the front door wide open, food from the fridge strewn all over the floor, and a big mess everywhere, so they guessed what had happened.

I was being held in a small cave in the *karanas* pit up the track at *Panapai.* The guy left to guard me, polished off the remainder of the brandy, and started to doze off. I made out I was already asleep. I sensed my time to escape was drawing nearer; I waited until he was snoring strongly, aware the other two may return at any moment. I removed my blindfold to see he was about a metre away from me, sleeping on his back with his hand on the bush knife across his chest. I managed to undo my hand ropes; then it was easy to remove the ones binding my legs; I unsteadily stood up, flexing my unresponsive hands and legs to get the blood circulating. He was sleeping right across the front of the small cave, which meant I had to step over him onto dry, dead leaves. *CRUNCH*, the noise seemed deafening; he must wake up!; I held my breath and listened to his snoring, then took another unsteady step. *CRUNCH*, the noise would wake the dead.

Fortunately, the alcohol had taken effect, he was out to it, carefully I picked a track through the dry leaves, stopping and listening for his snoring, but he was in a deep sleep, then when I was out of earshot, I ran for it. The area was dense jungle, and I headed through it for the high school; I knew if he woke up, he would assume I had gone down the track. I was barefoot, but I ran flat on through the bush; the ground had sharp coral protruding through, but I felt no pain with adrenaline pumping. I had put about a kilometre between myself and the *karanas pit* when I burst from the bush, startling four girls tending the *UTU High school vegetable garden*. I must have looked like *"Big Foot"* I only had a pair of stubbies shorts on, was barefooted, covered with sweat, dirt, and foliage, and my hands were bleeding from the spikes of the *"wait a while Kanda."* (cane) I was gasping for breath from my run through the jungle, the eyes of the startled girls darted, looking for an escape route from this wild man. I managed to convince them I would not harm them, and as I got my breath back, I explained what had happened, how I was kidnapped by *hardcore raskols* who had escaped from the *kalabus*. How I had just run from them, and would they please go and get my friend the Headmaster, *Mr Thompson*, while I hid in the garden in case the *raskols* had somehow followed me.

The garbled story Geoff Thompson got from the girls that morning was, *"your friend Andy Fletcher has escaped from the Kalabus; he is hiding up in the school garden and wants to see you."* Geoff drove up to the garden in his Landcruiser, wondering what the bloody hell was going on. I asked him to take me into the police station in town, and I filled him in on what had happened as we drove. When we came to *Fiscol,* I could see three police cars on my front lawn, so we went in.

A senior police officer from Port Moresby was in charge; he told me we had to get back to the *karanas pit* as quickly as possible. Hoping the guy would still be asleep, we sped down to where the track left the main road and walked in silently. I pointed out to them where I had left him sleeping; the police told me there would be two shots; the second would be the warning shot. They silently crept into the *karanas pit*, but the guy had long gone.

One of the Panapai villagers told us that my car came back from town with the two guys in it, then a few minutes later came careering down the track at high speed. They turned down the road away from town and headed towards *Namatanai*. They must have found both of us gone from the *Karanas pit*, And had panicked. The guy left to look after me must have woken up, and I was gone; knowing the police would be turning up very soon, he had run away and hid in the bush. The Police put a roadblock up at Namatanai and caught the two in my car later that day. They also put a *"toksave"* out that the guy who was still hiding in the bush near *Kavieng* would be shot on sight by Police, so he wisely walked back into the prison and gave himself up.

After they were all caught, I had to identify them in a line up at the Police Station; this was easy as I had a good look at all three; they did not try and hide who they were. Even If I hadn't recognised them, it would still have been easy to identify them, as all three were still wearing my jeans they had stolen. There was no doing this anonymously through a one-way mirror; I had to stand right next to them and point at their faces as the police took photos. I Later went to their Trials at the Kavieng Courthouse, where they each received a small extension to their already long-existing sentences.

During the whole kidnap ordeal, I always felt there would be a time when I would escape, especially after they started drinking heavily; it was only a matter of taking the chance when it presented itself, which I did. I had the Provincial Authorities seek me out and apologise to me for what had happened, telling me this was not the *Niuailan way*; these criminals were from *Goilala* and *Sepik*; they were not from *Niuailan*.

I dined out on the story for quite some time; everyone in *Niuailan* had heard about it. I would be stopped in the street by villagers, and wide-eyed kids, imploring me to tell the story of being *"hands-upped by the raskols."* I naturally embellished the story just a little, enjoying my celebrity status while it lasted. I told how a dozen raskols jumped me under my House and how I *kung-fu'd* ten of them, but the weight of numbers eventually wore me down. Everyone saw through my attempts at being macho and jokingly commented, *"I tin emi Bruce Lee ia,"* they all went away chuckling to themselves. I also had to recreate what had happened at the *karanas pit* for *Danius,* some of his friends from Lemakot, and *Johnny Korong;* when they came for the weekend, Johnny lived nearby at *Panapai.*

One Sunday morning, I was having a sleep-in; *Danius* and his friends playing 8-ball under the house, when I heard someone yelling out that a house was on fire. I didn't take any notice; I thought they were playing around. But the calls got louder; I jumped out of bed and went out onto the deck to see a house on fire. It was the lecturer's house who was away in Japan. And had thick smoke billowing from under the eaves. The wife had left a frying pan full of oil turned on and gone underneath the house to do some washing, the oil had ignited, and the fire spread rapidly through the wood-framed fibro house.

I grabbed my fire extinguisher and started to run up the stairs, but the fibro wall started exploding, so I retreated; the fire brigade arrived swiftly and went to start their water pump but found it had no fuel. They sped off back into town to find the Works Manager to unlock the Works yard, to get some fuel. When they returned to the College about half an hour later, they were far too late they found a pile of smouldering ruins. Not deterred, two groups of firemen rolled out their hoses and raced around to opposite sides of the embers and signalled for the pump to start up.

As it started up, the hoses filled with water, one crew squirted straight across the top of the embers to the other unit, knocking the helmet off the head of a fireman. The large crowd of kids that the fire had attracted fell about laughing at the fire truck crew's performance. The team undeterred, dampened down the pile of embers, then obviously satisfied by their efforts, drove off.

The Lecturer in Japan wanted to return home because his house had burned down, but the Administration didn't want him to come back. He used the fire as an excuse to come back because he was homesick but returned anyway despite being told to finish his course, so he lost his job when he turned up for work. Meaning my one-year temporary transfer from Vudal turned into a nine-year stint at the Fisheries College, where I spent time acting deputy and acting Principal.

Some of the *drug Bodies* that lived at *Miaom village*, adjacent to the College, watched my kids and students playing eight-ball under my house. They saw the table was a pay machine but didn't realise that the money part wasn't connected and all the games were free, they decided they would break into it to steal the coins.

One night I heard some shuffling feet under the house, but being wary about going down, after the last time, I waited until morning before going outside. They had carried the heavy table down to the garden to break into the money box. Feeling dumb and stupid after finding out the table did not have a money box, they took it out on the table by slashing the felt cloth. I got the students to help bring the table back under the house; then I bought some second-hand snooker cloth from *Harry Fong* at the *Kavieng Club* to repair it.

The Kavieng Club was where I spent most of my spare time; it was the old Colonial Planters club, which like the New Guinea Club in Rabaul, had racist, and sexist policies, during the Colonial times. No Local people had been allowed to join, and even white women were not allowed in the Bar. After Independence, these rules had to be changed, and the local members elected me onto the Committee to serve seven years as Honorary President to do this.

I rewrote the Constitution and passed it at a marathon Annual General Meeting, and in consultation with the members, I provided sporting and leisure activities for all the members. During my time as President, we amalgamated with the Golf Club, which was on the other side of the golf course. We initially used the golf clubhouse for dances and later turned it into offices for *Lihir Mining*, the money from the rental of these offices paid for the golf course maintenance.

We were using the Golf club building for Friday night dances; I counted the takings and did a stocktake of the beer and spirits. Stocktake was done around 11 am on Saturday after the dance. While the books always balanced, we never seemed to have much of a turnover.

So one Saturday morning after the dance, I did the stocktake at 9 am and uncovered the *barman's scam*; the stock was down a dozen cartons. The barman had taken out of the takings, the amount received from the sale of twelve cartons of beer over the bar, and then paid cash for twelve cartons at the beer wholesaler, thus pocketing the profits for himself. The day I did the early stocktake, the wholesaler had not yet delivered the replacement twelve cartons, thus exposing the barman's little earner. After that, we closed the Golf club as a drinking establishment and started on the renovations to turn it into offices.

The Kavieng Club had a kitchen that provided lunch and Tea. I and many others spent long hours playing snooker, watching Satellite TV, or just propping up the bar and would inevitably have an attack of the *munchies*. I got a *kai bar* built next to the Bar, which was continually being replenished throughout the day by Andrew, our cook. It sold fresh, locally caught fish, chips, red sausage, chicken wings, etc. To feed the customers during marathon sporting or social sessions. We also had the lunch and tea blackboard menu to choose from during the dining room hours, which sometimes included some dubious meals, such as *"Roast Lamp"* and *"Fork Chops."*

Joe Hiob was a good friend of mine who worked for *Gavin Yip*. He was a big guy and had a fearsome reputation, though he was a really nice guy to his friends. I arranged with Joe that the club would pay his annual membership fee if he would back me up as a bouncer at dances, or darts nights, when non-members may get a little rowdy. If someone was causing trouble, I would signal for Joe to accompany me, as he was always there playing snooker; I would then confront the drunken trouble-maker. Joe would be towering over my right shoulder, smacking the heavy end of his cue into the palm of his hand. Unsurprisingly the offenders always left the establishment straight away, closely followed by Joe, to make sure they went outside the main gate. Joe also loved the Billy Ray Cyrus song *"Achy Breaky Heart,"* when it was his turn to play in a snooker competition, he would always request that I play that song on our music P.A system. I was never quite sure if playing the piece was to motivate Joe to play better or to put his opponents off! Joe sadly passed away at only forty years of age in the early 2000s; *RIP Joe.*

Among my duties at the College, I was also the Transport officer; staff needing transport for their College excursions or the waterfront would write their requests on the Transport Noticeboard for their classes. I would then allocate the Truck, 26 seater bus, or the 12 seater bus, accordingly. Out behind the College was a chicken farm owned by a guy named Peni, and *Phyllis,* our Jamaican General Studies teacher, requested transport to take her business studies students there for an excursion. She wrote on the board, asking for a vehicle to Peni's Farm, some wag had then rubbed out the apostrophe, so I only saw a request to go to the Penis Farm. I went to Phyllis to ask where this place was, saying I might be interested in a bigger one; she did not get the joke until she saw the blackboard, then nearly wet herself, insisting she had put the apostrophe in place.

Danius had a wantok from Watara, named *Walter,* who was a student at Utu High School. Walter was a skinny little kid who seemed to be quite pleasant; he soon started hanging around with *Danius* and the other Duke kids from Lemakot on the weekends. Walter lived with his sister, who was married to a Namatanai but was a full-time border at Utu. His sister wanted him to go back to the DOY Islands as she couldn't afford his school fees. At the Club one day when I was drinking with *Geoff Thompson,* and *Jim Austin,* who were Headmaster and Deputy at Utu, they told me that Walter was about to be suspended for non-payment of his school fees. I told them not to do that, I would pay the outstanding amount, and again the following year, I spent the full amount.

Walter seemed very polite, helped with the household chores when staying with Danius, and was always respectful. Apparently, at school, though, it was a different story; he was a bit of a terror; *Geoff* would report on Walter's latest escapades when we would meet up for an afternoon drink at the club. I would talk to Walter when he came on the weekends, and he promised to be good, but his bad behaviour continued at the school until eventually, the Board of Management decided to expel him. Geoff told me that the best way was to withdraw him; before being expelled, I would get a partial refund of his school fees. I talked to Walter about it; he didn't seem worried that he would be removed, so I withdrew him and sent him down to his sister at Namatanai. I continued to sponsor many kids through School in PNG, and happily, the vast majority had a much better attitude towards schooling than Walter did.

Lemakot, where Danius was schooling, was about a 45-minute drive down the Highway, but because of lack of space, the Vocational Training Centre was being transferred to *Fissoa,* about a half-hour further on. Danius told me that there was this nice picnic spot on the river, at the place where they were going to build the new Centre. This Place which was called *"Wara Bulau,"* surrounded by virgin bush, the river which flowed out of the base of a limestone bluff about 300 yards upstream, was icy clean water

We went there for many picnics, the water was very refreshing to swim in on a hot day, and later when the Centre had been built and was in full swing, we were still welcome to drive through the school to the picnic area. It was here that I met *Brother Dan,* who had been Danius' teacher since he started at Lemakot, the brothers erected a *Haus Win* and permanent bbq at *Wara Bulau,* and it still is a popular picnic spot for Kavieng residents.

O a Sunday, driving down the road, a pig shot out right in front of me; I could not avoid it and was dragged along under the car for a bit. I saw it limp off into the bush. The next day I had a delegation from the village, led by my ex-apprentice from Rabaul Boroko motors, *Nick Kavok,* come down to the workshop in town to see me. I thought they were after compensation, so I immediately went on the offensive, telling them their pig wrecked the exhaust on my car, as well as denting the front mudguard. Nick, who was still an excellent friend of mine, said they were not worried about the pig, they had cooked it, and the women were at the market selling it as we spoke. They said that pigs were supposed to be fenced in Niuailan, it was their fault, was my car alright. I told them not to worry; my car was fine. Sally was a Canadian feminist who came as a General Studies Teacher to replace Phyllis. Sally was very loud and opinionated; she hated it when she told one of our male students to do something. The student would then turn to me for confirmation that it was alright to do it. She hated how the PNG culture was so male-oriented. She also would ask me how I made the students laugh, as she had told them jokes, and nobody laughed.

Sally had purchased a dog which she doted on, she named him *Rocky*, and *rocky* went everywhere Sally went. Sally had come up to my class one day to ask me to pass a message onto the students about transport for the excursion during the following lesson. Half the students would be going in the truck and the other half in the big bus. As Sally walked back down the stairs, I told the students half the class would go in the bus with Sally, and the other half would go in the truck with *Rocky*. The students erupted in laughter and stopped Sally in her tracks on the stairs, *"what did you say"* she mouthed as I looked out the window; I just shrugged. She asked me afterwards what I had said to make them laugh like that; I just told her it was a male thing, which I knew would make her cross.

Sally joined the Club and tried to organise people to play various games and social activities, when all they wanted to do was have a quiet drink, so she got up peoples nose a bit, after a while, everybody tried to avoid her as much as possible.

One evening she was walking home from her office. Two *raskols* who had been spying on the Girls Dorm tried to pull her into the bushes. She screamed out to the girls, who came running out, and the *raskols* ran away. The girls came and got me, as Sally was too scared to leave the dorm. We took her to her house, and the girls stayed with her for a while until she calmed down.

Next night I told *Geoff Thompson* in the bar of the Club, about Sally, Geoff asked, *"was everything okay, do you think there was any psychological damage done."* I reassured him, *"No, it appears both raskols have recovered from their ordeal okay."* It, cracked the bar up, as everyone knew Sally and nodded in agreement, *raskols* were undoubtedly game to take Sally on.

Margaret Cartland was a barmaid at the club; one night, she was working, she excused herself to go to the toilet; she was soon back in the bar, in a bit of a state. I asked her what was wrong, and she said, *"It was awful; as I went to the ladies toilet, someone shoved their thing through the fence."* I asked her, *"did you know the guy? Where was he from?" she* replied, *"Oh, I don't know I never looked at his face!!!"*

One year instead of going overseas on holiday, I used the money to buy a boat, and as there was nothing for sale in Kavieng, I enquired at the Rabaul yacht club about any boats for sale. I decided on a Caribbean 5.3-metre half-cabin, with the original sunshade, front seating, and a 100-litre under-deck fuel tank. I flew over one weekend and inspected *"Moonshiner,"* powered by an old *115 H.P. Suzuki*, which did seem to run okay. So as the owner threw in a game fishing chair, I decided to purchase it. Initially, I intended to drive the boat over to Kavieng, but an extended spell of bad weather, made me change my mind, and I got it shipped over on a barge.

The boat changed my lifestyle. Instead of going down the road for my Sunday picnics, I now went out on my boat to one of the many Tigak islands, I soon got to know the people on the various islands, and I was always welcome as I had plenty of BBQ food and drink.

I learnt of all the passages through the reefs and where I was allowed to go and not go; from the locals, they showed me how to line up prominent landmarks behind me to find the passage through the reef. I would always pick up kids from the islands to act as *"boskru,"* as we trolled for mackerel and rainbow runner. One island, in particular, *Nusalamon*, had only one family living on it; they told me I was always welcome to picnic or even overnight there, the family would join us for a BBQ lunch.

I spent seven Easters in a row camping on *Nusalamon Island*, at night with the full moon; I saw why the sea there was called *"Silver Sound"* on the chart, we would have a big bonfire on the sand spit at night, and the kids would dive for *kindams* (crayfish). I would sit under the stars in the balmy night air, once again eating fresh crayfish straight from the sea, washed down by a glass of chilled wine or cold beer, and wonder if life could get any better. There was also an island up a mangrove reach protected by a coral reef, rocks, and shallow water, where wild rock oysters thrived. The kids named this island *Andy Island*; they couldn't believe I ate the oysters raw, with only lime juice and a seafood sauce.

Andy Island had a small hill covered in kunai grass, which offered a nice view of the surrounding islands. Heading out on a Sunday morning before the breeze got up, the sea would always be like glass as the boat skimmed over the surface. I would stand on the bow where you could look down on the reef twenty metres below through the clear water to see turtles, manta rays, sharks, and fish of all description.

I took some students out to *Djual island* for a field trip; the sea was calm as we sped towards the island; we came across a whale-shark, basking in the sun on the surface, and then a pod of humpback whales. I slowed down to watch the whales frolic; they came over to us and dived under my boat. But having seen films of whales coming up underneath boats and smashing them to pieces, I decided to move on. I was privy where the yellow-fin tuna spawned; the calm bay would be seething with enormous fish; I had to slow right down to drive through them to prevent killing any.

The Tigak islands were lovely coral atolls with white sand beaches, Coconut palms and shade trees shading the beach from the hot tropical sun, truly Paradise on earth. Twelve years later, when I was again working in Kavieng, this time with no boat, A delegation from the islands Council came to see me. They were having problems on the islands with the youths causing trouble. They had nothing to entertain them, so they asked me if I would resume my picnics on the islands as when I had done this before, it had been a positive experience for the island kids, and the Village Elders had no trouble with them. I explained I no longer had a boat, so it would be pretty hard to resume my island picnics.

We had the Annual College picnic on *Ral island* one year, and I used my boat to ferry students along with the *MV Malagan* and the WW2 Vintage *MV Linde.* Some of the students were sitting on the back of my boat, which I anchored offshore. As the afternoon wore on, they were singing and moving around on the stern of the boat. They did not notice water was entering through the steering port. Before they knew it, water was halfway up the engine; we pulled the boat up on the beach and bailed it out. Water, unfortunately, had got inside the engine, and though I got it started straight away, corrosion was beginning to eat away internal metal parts of the machine.

I decided to buy a brand new Suzuki 140 H.P, which was the most powerful motor that would fit my boat's transom. I bought it from *Alan Jousiffe,* for cost price plus 5%, which was K5,000.00, less trade-in for my old motor of K1,000.00. I waited for the engine to be-assembled from the ground-up in Japan, and when it arrived, I had to run it in for ten hours before I could open the throttle fully to find out what it could do. I had made a slipway out of old railway lines, at the waterfront, for my boat; as a student project, there was a hand winch, which was very hard to wind up. I would always wind the boat down, then tell the students who acted as *boskru;* they had to do their share by rewinding it up when we came-in.

In 1987 Danius and James, a friend and wantok, and I travelled through Queensland, NSW, to my home state of South Australia. This trip was good, except Danius wanting to go to *Kings Cross* in Sydney on *New Year's Eve.* I told him of the dangers of this sleazy place, trying to protect him from the *Drug Bodies, Prostitutes,* and other assorted criminals that hung around there. Danius defied me and went by himself, he was eighteen and was getting strong headed at that age, so I couldn't persuade him not to go. When he returned, he looked shocked and didn't want to talk about what happened there.

Danius had met Agatha when he was a student at *Lemakot*; she was a Primary school teacher and was older than him. He got married to her when he was nineteen and moved to her village of Tembin on the west coast of Niuailan. They had three girls before they had a boy called *Fletcher;* at least one of the girls has married and has children. Agatha got transferred to a school on Lihir, and Danius got a job with the landowner company. I lent Danius the money to build his house at Tembin, which he repaid over time; when I was in Kavieng, I saw

Danius and the kids; I try and keep in touch as much as possible, despite the distance and communication problems.

One of my many duties at *Fiscol* was to go to Port Moresby every year to select our students for the next intake. Selections are done in a hall with the other higher learning institutions. I had to go through the comments on the student's reports and check their Exam results. Fortunately, there was a code that the school Principals used, which allowed us to read between the lines regarding student character. For example, *"Tries Hard"* means pretty hopeless, *"Has overcome his discipline problems"* means bad news. For girls, *"she is a mature girl"* means big breasts, and *"pleasant, and helpful"* means not good academically.

Alan Jousiffe, Roland Allbrook, Jim Austin, and Geoff Thompson had purchased a similar boat to mine though theirs was in an inferior condition. They had purchased a new motor, so even though the boat didn't look too good, it could get along okay. They used it to go out fishing, though *Geoff* preferred to drink, one day when Alan had pulled in a small reef shark. He started belting over the head to kill it; the shark swung around and took a chunk out of his cheek. The shark bit Alan, he was okay, but the shark died.

One Saturday afternoon, as I was relaxing at the club bar, Alan came in toting a large Marlin he had just caught; he was pretty chuffed with himself, propping it on a barstool and pronounced it was *"Marlin Monroe."* I was a bit suss, as it looked more like *"Marlin Brando"* to me. He was happy to leave it there until we told him to take it away.

When I became President of the club, I also took on the job as *Cricket Captain*; we had an annual match against the *New Guinea Club*. Furthermore, social matches against the Australian Navy Patrol boats that did regular exercises from Cairns to Kavieng. These games followed a dance the night before, and we're very social, no LBW, you had to retire after thirty runs, and you were allowed to field with a beer in hand. I had an Elephant cap that had a trunk on it that dangled down to my waist; I would bat in this, looking very serious; the bowlers, however, found it hard to concentrate. I would bring a couple of *the Papuan students,* from *Fiscol,* who could bowl pretty fast, to liven things up, but most of these games ended up diplomatically in a draw.

I played golf most Sunday mornings with *Roger Daulby,* the Public Works Manager; he was the only other golfer in Kavieng who was at my level of skill; this was more of a lower level than a higher level of skill.

We would have to fortify ourselves on the nine holes, which took us about four hours to complete. There was always the same five caddies that would turn up, two to carry the esky with the cold drinks and ice, one to hold my glass of Brandy and dry, one to take my clubs, and one to carry Roger's clubs. We didn't worry about the score much and used creative accounting for our score-cards. One time I hit my ball into the base of one of the large rain trees that dotted the course; I saw it was in a terrible lie but didn't have time to improve it before a caddy came along and found it. *"That's your ball,"* he said, *"No it's not,"* I said, *"yes it is,"* he said defiantly, as he tried to see the number on the ball. I went over and picked up the ball, studied the number, then declared, "Oh yes you are right, it is mine," and dropped the ball down a metre from the rain trees roots. *"Bai mi kotim yu lo Roger,"* (I'll tell Roger) said the caddie, catching me cheating; Roger, though was watching what was going on, from where his ball had landed in the rough and was in stitches already.

The Kavieng golf course is in two halves, and to play the back half, you have to walk down the road a hundred metres past the Police Station. I would make sure a caddie, who was about twelve years old, held my Brandy and dry glass as our Safari strode past the Police station front counter. The Duty Police would see us coming and go out the back for a drink of water or smoke as we went by; they never seemed to see us!! They were all members of the club and didn't want to upset the President.

As my third three-year contract was coming to an end, I decided I needed a change of scenery, so I indicated to the Department that I wouldn't be seeking a new contract. I also had been offered a job as the *Principal at Raval* starting in January 1995 and remembering the great times I had at Raval nineteen years previously, I had accepted. The Department said that if I stayed on for three more years, I would be Deputy Principal's substantive position at *Fiscol,* but I had made up my mind. I had six months to wait before they needed me at Raval, so I went back to *Bali, Thailand, and Penang* for an extended holiday.

I arrived back in Rabaul in September 1994 on a Friday afternoon and stayed with David Loh at New Britain Lodge. I told everyone how volcanoes were erupting where ever I had been. On Sunday night, David woke me with the news me we had to evacuate Rabaul as the volcano Tavurvur was about to erupt.

Tavurvur and Kalamanagunan erupted early on Monday morning and wiped out most of Rabaul. It took me a week to get out of Rabaul to Kavieng, and I went from there to Darwin to stay with Ken Burridge. My job as Principal of Raval went up in smoke with the Eruption.

Chapter 9

Kiunga & Manus 1996/9

I applied for a job as Principal of a GTZ Vocational Centre when I was in Darwin, and they tasked me with straightening out Kiunga Vocational Centre. I was met at Port Moresby Airport by Education officials, who took me to the Lamana Motel to check-in, waited for me, then drove me to the Education office. There I was shocked to hear, the previous Principal was still on leave and did not know he was no longer the *Principal of Kiunga* and transferred to Balimo, a much smaller school. They were waiting for him to return, to tell him of his fate, and all of his belongings were still in the Principals house at Kiunga.

I flew off to Kiunga via Daru and Balimo. Air Niugini to Daru, then by MBA to Kiunga, as I disembarked from the plane in Daru and walked to the Arrivals Hall. It looked like the entire population of the island had turned out for the arrival of the Aircraft. They seemed a surly-bunch was staring back at me as I approached the terminal; I thought I wouldn't know anybody here, as I'd never been to Daru before. But I was wrong from the back of the crowd; someone yelled out my name, it was a couple of my ex-students from Fisheries College.

They worked for Daru Fisheries and asked if I was going to work in Daru. When I told them I was moving to Kiunga Vocational, they told me to check out the Department of Primary Industry office in Kiunga; it was full of my ex-students. The MBA flight took off for Balimo airstrip, a grassed area, with a bush material departure lounge between two lagoons; once again, the whole town turned out for our arrival. We then flew on to Kiunga, the River Port Town for the Gigantic OK Tedi gold mine, on the mighty Fly River. The port at Kiunga is over nine hundred kilometres upstream from the Fly River's mouth but only ten metres above sea level. From Kiunga, the ground rises to the rugged Star Mountains, up to the *OK Tedi Gold Mine* is situated; this a very high rainfall area, the annual rainfall is over 10 metres in a lot of places. *Kelly* my Deputy was there to meet me at the Airport in Kiunga; he was a short but pleasant Southern Highlander. He took me to my house, the Principal's house, the most prominent place on Campus; the house was full of the previous Managers belongings. I decided to spend the first couple of nights at the Guest-house in town. The lady teachers packed everything into one room and locked the door before I moved in. These personal belongings were picked up about a month later and transported to Balimo.

The house was high set and had many exotic fruit trees from the Philippines growing in its garden; it had verandah's on two sides, had three bedrooms, laundry and an entertainment area underneath the house. The humidity in Kiunga is the highest I've experienced in PNG; the inside walls were black from mould, even though they were washed down regularly with bleach. They had rivulets of water from the humidity running down them, my camera became a victim of the humidity very early on, so I never took many photos of Kiunga.

The School had girl students and boys, and we had a couple of outstanding female staff members. One of them ran the school canteen, which sold the goods made by the girls in their cooking and sewing classes. The store also sold basic foodstuffs, such as rice, Ox and Palm bully beef, and was run by the girls. I did a daily stocktake and counted the money. The girls also made cakes and scones for the Staff-room, which the staff enjoyed every day, except on Friday fortnight the Staff Room was eerily empty. I had the room and the cakes to myself as I fielded telephone call, after call, from family members of the Staff in Port Moresby, wanting money transferred to their bank accounts.

I wondered why all the other schools received money from the OK Tedi Mine through the Tax relief scheme, and we didn't. OK-Tedi spent money on classrooms and workshops for the Provincial schools, and this money deducted from their Tax Bill. I found out from Kelly that the previous Principal had been given money to rebuild an ablution block and had *"diverted"* the money to buy a Land Cruiser; this had resulted in the Mine dumping the school from the tax scheme.

I went to see the officials at the mine office and told them I was now in charge. Any money donated would be spent on the designated project. They agreed to give us another chance and donated money once again to rebuild the ablution block. I did a photo album on the building's progress for them, with a drawdown of the funds and copies of all the receipts. They came and inspected the facility then announced in their next budget; we would get new workshops, staff houses, and dormitories the following year. I don't know whether this happened, as I had transferred to Manus by then.

In my early days in Kiunga, I visited all the fast food outlets in town, looking for some fish, chips, red sausage, chicken wings, and legs, but all I found in all the trays were Sheep-Tongues, nothing else but sheep tongues. I decided to buy bread and tinned leg ham for lunch; I asked the students about the lack of choice, they said they liked sheep tongue, just as well that's all there was.

The two Supermarkets in town were both owned by the same company; the prices were outrageously high. Another option, a three and a half-hour drive up the well-maintained road, was Tabubil, a Company subsidised Supermarket for the mine-workers. Of course, I couldn't drive up to Tabubil every time I wanted a loaf of bread, so I did my grocery shopping in Kiunga, but every six weeks, I drove up to Tabubil to do my freezer shopping. The road to Tabubil was a Company road, and it had two graders working around the clock, maintaining it; there was also regular convoys of around 14 semi-trailers that travelled down it every three hours. These convoys had-right-of-way, so when you encountered a land cruiser belting down the road at speed with a big sign on the roof that said 14. You had to get right off the road and count the trucks that passed; after the fourteenth, which was the tyre-truck, you could resume your journey.

I used the school land cruiser for this trip, but after a couple of months, I purchased a second hand Police Blue Suzuki Jimny from a Doctor who was going-finish from the Hospital. The drive up to the mining town at Tabubil was a good break from Kiunga, they had a decent hotel appropriately called cloudlands, and the supermarket had a wide choice of very cheap prime cuts of meat. I usually took some students with me and would have lunch at the hotel, though I would give a swim in the pool a miss, as the altitude made the water look freezing indeed.

There were a couple of small towns on the road; *Ningerum* was one of them. It was on the top of a mountain, overlooking the Indonesian border just a few hundred metres away but hidden in the mist. The traditional border crossing was allowed, and often, you would see an Irian-Jaya tribesman, dressed only in a Penis-Gourd, when coming around a corner in the road. I would surprise them, walking on the straight stretches of the road in the distance; as soon as they heard or saw the car, they would disappear into the bush.

This part of PNG had the very dangerous Black Taipan snakes, known locally as the "*Papuan Black,*" one night I followed the cement path from the back of my house down to the shed to get something. Luckily I had a torch, which I was shining ahead of me, because there were two Papuan blacks curled up on the path, enjoying the residual heat in the cement; I turned around and went back inside the house.

David Loh sent over my crate, which had many of my personal belongings, which had been buried under ash from the volcanic eruption in Rabaul two years earlier. When I opened the crate, I was not expecting much, the sulphur smell reminded me of the eruption, but my silk shirts and Italian trousers looked okay. However, when

I washed them in the washing machine, all I ended up with was a machine full of rags, the most significant hand-sized pieces. Many of my photos were also ruined, though I managed to salvage about a quarter of them. I had already purchased a new Television and video player. And many clothes from Australia, Singapore, and Thailand, so I had already moved on from the 1994 Eruption.

A few of my friends back in Rabaul, though, couldn't let go of their pre-eruption lifestyle and enjoyed playing *"The Victim of the cataclysmic eruption,"* growing beards, smoking *"Brus"* the local tobacco, and generally looking scruffy. This nonsense didn't go on for too long, as they realised they had to cut their losses and move on. Brian was in New Zealand at the time of the eruption; he was fighting a debilitating disease and never returned to PNG.

We had many students from the Blackwater Refugee Camp attending the school, and they soon became attached to me, as I would address them in *Bahasa Melayu* at assembly. We would have long discussions on their predicament in the PNG Camp, and I could also practise my *Melayu.* They would come over to my house to do their washing in my Automatic washing machine, and we would try and solve the West Papua issue by ourselves.

Kiunga was not only a very humid place, but it had the most incredible electric storms; some of them late at night would have the sky lit up, the thunder was deafening. I would sit out on the balcony and watch the incredible sound and light show, as it was impossible to sleep through it. Quite often, the lightning would knock out the cables on the free satellite Television service, which was courtesy of the OK Tedi mine; the Technicians would be on the job first thing in the morning, so we would be back online in no time.

Like at all the schools I taught at, I always tried to get the students to be more involved with their school and be proud of it, so I purchased printed overalls. They were so proud of these; they would wear them all over town and down to the market. Even the High school kids across the road lined the fence to watch when my boys and girls wore their overalls for the first time.

In the middle of the year, there was an incident in town. A couple of guys from the Southern Highlands murdered a local guy in a drunken brawl at a club. With the PNG Payback system, no Southern Highlands person was safe from payback killings, including Kelly, my Deputy. He had moved out of his house and was hiding in one of our junior teachers' house. His wife was from Daru, so okay; his kids were also not targets.

The two Supermarkets and Westpac Bank were locked up and guarded by Riot Police. We would have run out of Rations, but fortunately, we had our store, so we got through alright. There was a roadblock on the Tabubil road, looking for Highlanders, but were also turning back all cars. Fortuitously for me, the President of the Board of Governors of my school was in charge of the roadblock. So I got through to restock my supplies from Tabubil. The situation quietened down as offenders got caught, and the two supermarkets were allowed to reopen under the police's supervision. Only six persons were allowed inside at once. The bank also reopened, so I could get out some money and go around and pay off my *"dinau,"* Kelly came back out of hiding, and the whole town slowly returned to normal.

OK Tedi had famously failed to build a proper tailings dam, the dodgy one they created failed, because of the massive rainfall in the catchment area of the mine. So the mine tailings, including heavy metals and cyanide, were left to flow down the Alice River. And into the Fly just below Kiunga. The mine paid out massive compensation for the loss of fish, and agricultural land, used for food gardens. The local people who lived away from the river moved down to the riverbanks and started food gardens to be eligible for compensation. These people would meet in our Staff Room to discuss their tactics; a few received Compensation they were not entitled to; the mine knew this but seemed happy to pay up to keep the peace.

The guy in charge of the Project for GTZ was an ex-British Army Major, and the second in command was a German, and they could not stand each other. The Boss came to visit me first and did not endear himself with me either; he assumed that because I had lived in the country for a while, I would be against any change in vocational training. But was not the case; I liked the idea he was promoting, of doing various short courses at the village level. His Deputy came to visit later; he was a nice guy, relatively young, but seemed competent; I held a staff BBQ for him under my house. He thoroughly enjoyed himself, chatting with the staff and their families and the head boy and girl; we seemed to get on quite well. After he had returned to Port Moresby, he rang me and told me the Major was going elsewhere and there would be a new Project Leader coming. It was right now that I had a friend in the Headquarters of GTZ to keep me informed on what was going on. Near the end of 1996, I applied for the Positions, *Principal, Raval, and Manus* to get back to the New Guinea Islands. I did hear from Raval, they had an excellent local Principal, and they were going to stick with him, but I did not hear from Manus at all. I went to Bali on leave, then returned six weeks later, to find there was still no reply from *Manus,* so I rang my friend at GTZ to ask him if he knew anything; he told me he would investigate and get back to me.

He rang me later that same day to tell me the Education Department had appointed me to Manus, but GTZ wanted me to stay at Kiunga, so they hadn't passed on the message. I was furious; I didn't work for GTZ; I worked for the PNG Government. I rang GTZ and told them I was going to *Manus,* they tried to talk me out of it, saying it was a smaller school, but I was cross. They were trying to manipulate me.

I rang through to the Education office in Lorengau in Manus and got the receptionist, I asked for the Assistant Secretary, but she told me everyone was meeting. So I asked her if she had the appointments list there. She said she did, and I asked her who was appointed Principal of the Vocational Training Centre; she said, *"Andrew Fletcher, tasol emi no kam."* I told her who I was and that I had only just found out about my appointment, and I would be taking the Position.

I packed up at Kiunga, feeling a little guilty about leaving them in the lurch, and headed for Manus. When I arrived in Manus, the Education Assistant Secretary was pleased to see me as the Manus Training Centre was in a massive mess. Each section of the school had their bank account, and the staff had been using it as their account. The Westpac bank had closed all accounts.

This situation was bread and butter for me, sorting out the team and the students.

I asked the Governor for K50,000 to renovate the school and set about turning the school around. I redid the students' dormitory, repainting and replacing broken fibro, fitting new flywire, and installing overhead fans. The ablution block was completely renovated from the ground up, and the mess had ceramic tiles laid and Satellite Television, with fifty plus channels installed. The old American Army World War two Quonset huts had all the corrugated iron replaced, and the workshops had new tools courtesy of GTZ.

I purchased new school uniforms from Singapore and banned students from having Rasta style haircuts or wearing caps during school hours. Students could not smoke on the school premises, but the older ones could go out on the road to smoke during the break; I got an immediate positive response from the students and a new nickname, *"Rait Man"*. I had to go to the bank, get the accounts sorted out, and open only one School account. The various money-making sections are given a budget every term to buy consumables; All sales had to be receipted and banked by me. It was the hardest thing for the staff to get used to, not boosting their teacher's wages with drum oven sales. It was a constant battle with a couple of the team, who thought their section was their private cash cow.

The Education authorities told me they wanted the Centre cleaned up, and they would fully support me. In most things, they did, but they dithered when it came to sacking corrupt or drunken staff. Because of the Wantok System, all the staff were somehow distantly related to Headquarters Staff, and they *"couldn't"* sack them

I also asked a Seargent Major from the Lombrum Naval Base to come on Friday Afternoons to teach marching during our sports sessions. It was very popular with the students; the marching music blared out as students learned new marching drills. The fence line around the school packed with residents turned out to watch the marching, yelling support, or otherwise if someone turned the wrong way.

The students responded well, and instead of being the poor cousin, suddenly *Manus Vocational Training Centre* was right up there with the other schools in the school's appearance and the students. The marching also had another unexpected benefit; all the students decided to wear short military-style haircuts, making them look pretty cool in their new uniforms. I gained the students' respect very quickly at this school; as the student body's benefits came thick and fast, I introduced girls into the school for the first time. GTZ paid to have a carpentry workshop turned into a home economics centre, with stoves, fridges, and sewing machines. They had to be day students, as we didn't have room for a female dorm, I also employed a lady teacher for this class, but she turned out to be a bit of a worry.

There was a Soccer tournament at the town playing fields, and we allocated to sell hot dogs. I bought a carton of red sausage, some bread buns, and tomato sauce. The saveloys were quite large, and we would have to sell them for three Kina to make a profit. So I told the lady teacher to slice them down the middle, put half a sausage in each roll, and sell them for Two Kina. After selling out, I counted the money when she came back with the takings and found we had made a substantial loss. I asked her if she had sliced the sausages down the middle; she said, *"Ol man ino laik."* !!!

My House in Lorengau was on the old market site. Along with a number of our workshops, and across the road. From the other staff houses, the main workshop, and the office area. Lorengau was a prominent American base during World War Two and covered by *Quonset huts,* some of which are still standing. Most of them have not survived apart from the cement slabs they stood on; most yards in Lorengau have cement slabs, my house being no exception. *David Loh* suggested I paint my slab green, and everyone would then think I had a neatly manicured lawn.

Every Saturday, Val Knight, Cyril, and I, had lunch at the *Lorengau Hotel* and were quite often joined by the Commander of Lombrum Base and any other visitor that might be staying at the hotel. These were great sessions and were the only times I drank alcohol in Manus, except for a few picnics, with the students. Management had instructed the girls that worked in the Restaurant at the hotel to tell any customer who inquired what type of fish was it in the Fish and Chips that it was *Red Emperor.* The Hotel purchased fresh fish from the local fishermen, and they bought a wide variety of reef fish. Having worked for the Fisheries College in Kavieng for nine years, I was quite familiar with the different reef fish species, taste, and texture. So as I had the Fish and Chips every Saturday, I would identify the fish species, and someone would then ask the girls what type of fish it was; it was our ongoing joke.

One day as we turned up for our Saturday lunch, there was consternation amongst the restaurant girls. I asked what the problem was and was told, *"Sori Mista Andy, we have no chips, so we've had to use cut up potatoes."* I said to them that this was not a problem; we could have cut up potatoes with our *"Red Emperor"* this time. They did not associate the chips, which came frozen in a twenty-kilo white plastic bag, with that brown root vegetable, the humble potato, from the ground. It became another of our ongoing jokes; someone would always ask, *"what do we have today, chips, or cut up potatoes?"*

We started the GTZ program doing short courses at the Village level in earnest, at Manus. I was a regular on *Radio Manus*, providing a weekly *Pidgin* update on what we were doing at the Centre, on the program *"Wanem samting I kamap long Manus."* (What's on in Manus) The studio would ring me at the Centre and interview me on the air in Pidgin, and I would be able to tell the audience where and when short courses were going to be. This communication method was so effective; we would sometimes have to run two or three courses in succession because of the large number of participants.

We did one week of courses on Trade Store Management, Pig, Poultry Husbandry, Tank making, Foundation laying, Outboard Motor Maintenance, Net Mending, and many other useful skills. In most cases, I used town residents, who were retired tradesmen or highly skilled persons, and my staff, as the course Instructors. The participants paid Five-kina each to take part, which went to the Instructors. The Centre, through GTZ, provided any consumables or tools needed to run the courses successfully; these courses were a great success and were very popular. Though they were not popular with my staff, they just saw it as extra work, for the same pay.

Val told me to stop hogging the radio; she said every time she turned it on, I would be ranting on about some course or other to be held up the highway or in a village.

GTZ was very happy with these courses' success, and the new German Project Manager was always coming to Manus to visit us, though he did spend a fair bit of his time out fishing. Manus was just two degrees south of the Equator, so it had a warm climate, and the fishing was excellent; I never bothered to go fishing myself, as you could buy cheap fresh fish at the town market. The favourite at the market was the smoked fish, but I preferred it freshly caught. I got my garden veggies and fruit supplies from the market and my freezer, bread, and other groceries from Steamships Supermarket.

Like quite a few I occupied in PNG, my House only had cold water to shower in; there was an overhead tank with a hand pump, which the students would pump up during the morning work parade. I painted my overhead tank matt black to absorb the sun's rays during the day, but the water would be icy during extended periods of wind and rain. I decided to use the *Indonesian mandi* system during these times; I purchased a large plastic rubbish bin and filled it with cold water. Before my shower time, I would add a couple of boiling water jugs to take the edge off the icy water and then use a plastic Mandi dipper to sluice water over myself.

For six months during my time in Manus, we had a drought, our water supply was from the river, so for washing and flushing toilets, we had no problem, but for cooking and drinking, we relied on two rainwater tanks at my house. After a couple of weeks, the other schools in town closed, but we could keep going until we ran out of drinking water. My staff were furious, wanting to sit on their bums at home and do nothing and get paid for it. I refused to close up, as we could still operate effectively.

Joseph, one of my laziest staff, reported me to the health inspector, who came and did a check on everything.

He reported that the river water had shell particles in it; I told him that it always did and was used only for flushing toilets and showers; so, no problem. At the urging of Joseph, he still wanted to close the school. I told him as the river water was always like that, he would have to shut us permanently. And the other schools in town as well. I pointed out to Joseph that he would then lose his job. The Health Inspector then decided it was okay for us to continue until we ran out of drinking water, which was my strategy in the first place. We got some heavy rain when the tanks got down to the last couple of rungs.

On some Sundays, I would take a number of my students for a picnic to the beaches of *Los Negros Island,* out past *Momote Airstrip.* There are two beaches there, *Salamei* on the Westside, and *"Aircon"* on the East. So no matter which way the wind was blowing, one of these beaches would have calm seas. *Salamei* I renamed Salami, and Aircon, the American troops' name, given to the other beach during WW2. I renamed *Ret Sosis* beach. (red sausage). I would bring lots of Ret Sosis, chicken wings, lamb flaps, onion and bread, with cordial. And a twelve-pack of beer for the older students to have under my supervision.

Drinking was a problem amongst my students, the Centre being in town meant they could meet up with friends and drink on the weekends. The students always drank to get drunk; I tried to show them they could enjoy a couple of beers and then stop, though I had limited success with my campaign. Initially, I also had trouble with drunken youths in town from *Long Island* who were sleeping in our *Dorm* on Saturday night. I was surprised at this, as *Long Island* was where my friend *Jessie Poloat* from Panguna Mine was a seven-day Adventist Island. Their religion tells them to abstain from alcohol.

The youths were disregarding their religion to take up drinking alcohol; the Long Island youth's drinking habits were none of my business. But when they got drunk and came into my dorm, causing trouble and sleeping there, it became my business. So on the advice of my Long Island Deputy Principal. I wrote a letter to the island Council, voicing my displeasure at the island youths' behaviour when in town. Requesting they tell them to stay away from my school. Surprisingly this worked, and I never had another drunken Long Islander turn up at my school, looking for a bed. My letter caused quite a stir on the island, but my friend Jesse. Who had retired to his home there spoke up on my behalf. Saying he knew me well and I wouldn't have written a letter like that if it wasn't a school problem.

During week-days I turned the tv off at 9 pm. *Outsiders* were also allowed to come into the mess to watch with my students. They also had to abide by the school rules when on the school property. Included no smoking; in the early days, some of the outsiders would smoke inside the Mess. When I came to lock up, I could smell the cigarette smoke. I would ask who was smoking; they usually showed respect enough to own up; I would explain the rules to them and tell them they could be banned if they continued to smoke. I had the full support of my students, and after a while, they would themselves stop outsiders from smoking. The *outsiders* showed great respect towards me and would always say good night as they left the premises.

I did have a problem at one stage when a small number of rations were going missing from the ration store, the ration store was very secure, so I thought someone must have a key. There was one tin of *Ox and Palm* Bully beef and two packets of beef crackers going missing every night. I changed the lock, knowing I would catch the offender. Experience had taught me that when people were stealing food and then stopped, the perpetrator would get hungry and come and complain that the rations were not enough. Sure enough, one of the prefects, who had access to the Ration store keys at times, complained about being hungry. I asked him for his keys and checked the old lock against his keys. A key fitted, he had to face the *Board of Governors* to get a dressing down but was allowed to stay on.

The Sea Kayaking world championships one year was in the waters around the Lombrum base. The Vocational Centre had to renovate some of the Quonset huts there to house the participants. We also got the contract to provide the general rubbish bin-stands around town. The Australian Lady, who was in charge of this event, also joined our session every Saturday, as she stayed at the hotel. She was going to be in Manus for six months and declared her desire to get Malaria. All of us who had suffered multiple doses of the mosquito-borne disease warned her about how debilitating it could be. But she insisted on sitting outside in the evenings when mosquitoes were most active. She did get Malaria and a nasty dose of it; she told us after she recovered that if she ever repeated anything as stupid as wanting to get Malaria, we were to slap her face!!

At the end of the first year at Manus, after all the students had gone home, I attended an official function at the Governor's residence; as I drove out of my house, I noticed one of my teachers in-laws sitting on the road. I knew these guys were from Long Island and had a bad reputation around town for breaking into houses. When I returned later that night, it was no surprise that someone had broken into my house, and my TV and Video player was missing. The next morning I reported the break-and-enter to the Police. There was quite a crowd at my home watching, including my teacher's wife, who was related to the suspects.

The Detective in my bedroom, looking for fingerprints, had his back to the window as he told me it was no good; the louvres were too dirty to get good prints. I could see the teacher's wife outside trying to overhear what he was saying, so I said in a loud voice, *"oh, that's great, you've got good fingerprints, we'll be able to catch them now,"* The teacher's wife looked shocked, and quickly left. The detective looked at me as if I was an idiot and started to repeat himself, but I stopped him with a finger over my lips as I told him about the woman listening.

The next day one of the suspects from the road came to see me saying he knew who had taken my TV and video, and for K100, he could get them back. I thought this would be the best option; even though I knew this guy stole them, I would never be able to prove it. So I went with him to a house in the *squatter settlement* and retrieved my goods for K100. I told the Police I had recovered my belongings, and they dropped the case. The detective asked me if my lie had worked. I told him *yes*, the suspect was the ladies brother, and he had told me to ask the Police to destroy the fingerprints; we got a good laugh out of that.

After two years at Manus, when my *Work Contract* was about to expire, I received a phone call from *Alan Jousiffe,* asking if I would be available to Manage his business in Kavieng the following year, 1999. Alan's kids were getting near high school age, and he wanted to move down south to Australia, where he had purchased a mango farm. I thought it was probably about time that I got back into Private Enterprise after 24 years in Education and training. So it was with a heavy heart that I rang the Overseas Staffing Unit in Port Moresby to tell them I would not be seeking another contract.

Chapter 10

Kavieng, Port Moresby. 1999/06

The previous twenty-four years had been the best years of my life; I had thoroughly enjoyed teaching, the PNG kids had been a pleasure and an honour to teach. It wasn't long before I had a phone call from The Governor telling me how he was so happy with what I had done at the *Manus Vocational Training Centre,* and would I please reconsider. I told him I had no new contract, and he told me not to worry about that as he would ensure I got a new deal. I told him I had accepted a job in Kavieng; he told me he was so sorry to see me go but wished me luck.

After five years, I was happy returning to Kavieng, as I had enjoyed my nine-year stint at the *Fisheries College.* This time though, I would be with *Private Enterprise* and not with *Government Education and Training.* It was going to be different. To start with, I did not have ten weeks of holiday a year, but I would have to get used to it.

I had a comfortable high set three-bedroom house opposite the *Kalabus* (Prison), which was only five minutes drive to work. And the use of a red sporty *Mazda 323* with petrol provided, so was pretty well set up. I was elected *President of the Kavieng Club*, again as many of the National members from my time before were still members. But there were some trashy new *whities*, though some good ones like Dave Thorold and *Gary Lawson* remained. *Dave Thorold, aka Animal,* was renowned for eating cockroaches and being good with his fists when provoked. We always drank together in the Bar; Dave had mellowed somewhat as he had grown older, he doted on his daughter, who would accompany him to the club to wait for him.

The Kavieng Club Bar was starting to show its age. The floor was beginning to rot, and we were in danger of losing a bartender through the rotting timbers. So the Committee approved renovations; we used Rex, a local carpenter who was also an active member of the club, using my plans and supervision. Having frequented many bars throughout PNG, I combined some of them' features to come up with a plan for the new bar. The plan's part was the enlarged bar area for the dance and function side; previously, this area had been tiny. We purchased four large security mesh roller shutters, made to order at a low price thanks to *Regent,* the renovations took a while, but it was a vast improvement when finished. We still had the income from Lihir Mining Offices at the old *Golf Club Building*, but the golf course maintenance was an ongoing issue; it was expensive to maintain the course. The golfers didn't help by not wanting to pay much for green fees but expect expensive prizes when they won a monthly medal or some such. I continued to promote junior golf, the club's future, as many senior golfers were getting a bit long in the tooth. The senior golfers didn't like it much when junior golfers paid full fees and played against the seniors, as the juniors nearly always won.

Champion African American golfer *Tiger Woods* was a great role model for the PNG junior golfers and caused a massive upsurge in golf interest. We held the PNG Junior championships in Kavieng one year, with junior golfers from all over the country. We were so short of accommodation I had to put up half a dozen of them in my house. Here, I met Eremas Pepem representing *Ralum Club in Kokopo*; Eremas told me his story, how his dad had abandoned him and the rest of his family, including his mum Margaret. When he went back to Kokopo, I told him that I would sponsor him in Golf Tournaments; he seemed to be a keen golfer and have good skills. A few months later, Margaret turned up in Kavieng with Eremas, fifteen at the time. Margaret's mother was from *Kulangit*, a Village near Kavieng; she claimed her Mothers land, New Ireland, is a Matrilineal Society.

It wasn't long before Margaret, and I teamed up; she was thirty-five at the time, roughly the same age as me, *cough*!. Then over from Kokopo came the rest of the family, Colleen, aged 14, Ephraim, aged 11, Talom aged 9, and Elipas, a toddler. It was a package deal; Margaret spent most of the time at Kulangit, as there was some resistance to her getting any land. Eventually, I purchased a land block at *Kulangit Blocks* and registered it in her name with the Lands Department. Margaret had struggled to provide for the kids. The fathers had not committed to providing any support for her. She had only been able to afford to put Eremas into Community school; the others had not yet been to school. The first thing I did was to enrol the school-age kids in school. Because they survived on fried flour mixed with water and what garden vegetables Margaret could grow, the protein was a rare luxury. I could improve on this straight away; all the meals I provided were balanced; the nightly meals were mostly nutritious. Two kilos of chicken wings. Or lamb forequarter chops, sweet potato, potato, onion, Chinese cabbage, beans, two cans of diced tomatoes, garlic, pepper, salt, and chicken stock cubes. All cooked up in my gigantic wok and served with a kilo of *Trukai rice* cooked in my Rice Cooker, one of the boys had won at golf.

Colleen settled with Margaret in Kulangit, and Eremas, Effie, and Talom moved into my house; Talom was not sure about living in the big house as he was shy. It took him six weeks before he would even talk to me. He would smile at my jokes but not say a thing. As he became accustomed to me, he became more relaxed, until one day, I got cross with him for doing something wrong and told him to go and stay with his mum for a while at Kulangit. He refused, and as I locked him out of the house, he built himself a little cubby on the back landing where he was going to sleep. I finally relented at ten o'clock that night and let him in. He went to his room, and when I went to talk to him, he wouldn't let me in; I forcibly pushed the door open, grabbed him and gave him a huge hug.

From that day on we were best mates, we were inseparable, when he had a bike accident and opened a big gash on his forehead. I took him down to the hospital, where he gripped my hand so tightly as the nurse put a dozen stitches in without anaesthetic. He would also accompany me to the club whenever I would allow him. One day, as we drove past the Court-house oval, a gaggle of fat dumpy middle-aged women were playing soccer. With mature breasts swinging like pendulums, they lumbered after the ball like a herd of buffalo, pushing and shoving each other out of the way to get a boot to the ball.

Not being a fan of women playing men's sport, I muttered under my breath, *"Ol meri I mas got bol ia."* (those ladies must have balls) Not realising Talom had picked up on what I had said. Later that day, as Talom and I took Margaret back down to Kulangit, we passed the oval, where the ladies were still in hot pursuit of the soccer ball, though they did seem to have it surrounded. Talom piped up, telling his mum, *"ol meri I gat bol, laka Dad."* (Those ladies have balls, isn't that right, Dad?) Margaret was shocked and scolded him; he looked at me for support as, after all, it had been me that had said that. I couldn't let him cop the blame and *fessed up,* telling Margaret I was only mumbling to myself and would be more careful in the future, but also, it was true.

I got all the kids into school, as only Eremas had been to *Kalamanagunan Community School* in Kokopo. Ephraim and Talom went just across the road to the Corrective Community School Eremas and Colleen to Sacred Heart. I had a lot of trouble with Eremas at school; he seemed to have similar problems as Walter at UTU.

Eventually, I removed Eremas and Colleen from Sacred Heart, and all of the kids were enrolled at *Kaselok Community School*, about half an hour's drive down the highway. Eremas had a friend at school called <u>Trevor Maino,</u> whose mum was from Manus. She worked on the checkout at *Bisi Trading* in town; his father had split with his mother and worked in Port Moresby. Trevor and his small brother *J.O.* lived with their mum in *Broken City*, a squatter settlement on the outskirts of town,

Trevor was a very bright kid but had trouble doing his homework as they had no power or running water, so he moved in with us at his mother's request. Later, J.O. joined him and *Kasimir, Paul, Norbert*, and various other nomadic tribespersons. I had up to a dozen mouths to feed at times; some things just never changed.

At Regent, we had many customers from the Kontu area on the Central West Coast area of New Ireland. They requested that we sponsor the Shark calling festival held for the first time at their village. I drove down with a couple of my Madak staff and Ephraim and Talom; the festival had many traditional dances. And the canoes going out for the conventional shark calling. A European film crew wanted to film everything as if it was the first time this remote tribe had contact with white people. And me wandering into their shots everywhere doing my official duties spoiled their plans.

I told them to bugger off, with their condescending attitude was not welcome as the people of Kontu were not a primitive tribe. They had a Mazda T3500 Truck which they had purchased from us, and they drove into town a couple of times a week for supplies. They had an official viewing platform for VIP guests; I had to open the festival, give a speech, and provide lunch. The French film crew went about their business, but I'm sure they planned to edit me out of any of their footage. So they could portray the Kontu people as a *"lost tribe,"* they would also have to edit out the vehicles and P. A. system.

Alan Jousiffe and his wife Mary, who owned Regent, had moved to Mareeba just outside of Cairns where they had purchased a Mango farm; Alan would visit every couple of months to see how his business was going. For the first four years, I was at Regent, Paul Tohian was Governor, and we benefitted from Mazda Vehicles' sale to the Provincial Government. We also had a maintenance agreement with them and a constant income source for the Company. Public servants driving whilst drunk and smashing up the vehicles, and Jealous wives smashing all the glass in the cars after suspecting their husbands were not faithful, were frequent events. Brian Dicker was the Spare Parts Manager, a naturalised citizen, he was married to a Namatanai girl; Brian had a wonderful sense of humour and gave me generous support. I had someone come and tell me one day that a couple of my spare parts staff had tried to sell him a brand new Stihl chainsaw at a low price. I saw Brian, who told me we only had one left in stock; we went to the section where the Chainsaw box was still in the right place on the top shelf but found it was empty. I questioned the two staff members individually and told them they were looking at ten years in prison for stealing from their employer. One of them confessed and told me what had happened.

He and the other suspect were cleaning up in the spare parts section; there was no one else around, so they removed the 090 Stihl chainsaw worth around K6000.00. from its box. They put it in the bin they were filling with rubbish, covered it up and took it outside to the skip; they came late that night to retrieve it. They took it around town, asking people, including my informant, to buy it for K1,000.00 but got no takers. I asked him where the chainsaw was and went with him to pick it up; I then dropped the two at the Police Station and asked them to be charged with stealing.

The two went to court, where the Magistrate decided since Regent had recovered the stolen property, he would let the two suspects off. I couldn't believe it. But even worse, the two thieves came to see me asking for their jobs back because the Magistrate had let them off. That did not happen; it was a constant battle preventing stealing from the workshop and spare parts.

Another new staff member in the spare parts was *"selling"* goods to customers cheaply, not writing a receipt and pocketing the money. He was found out pretty quickly by selling a car battery to a customer, not realising it had no acid in it. The customer returned with the car battery the next day for the acid. The shonky parts salesman was having a day off to spend his ill-gotten gains. The customer then went to one of our honest staff who asked for the battery's receipt, and the scam exposed; the Police arrested and charged the dodgy staff member.

We also had people climbing over the fence into our yard late at night, looking for things to steal, not realising that we had two large German Shepherd dogs roaming the yard at night. On more than one occasion, when I came into work, there would be someone standing in the tray of a truck bailed up by the dogs. On these occasions, the Police collected them after the dogs were chained up. Regent had sixty-five staff in two locations, Kavieng and a small operation on *Lihir Island*, the home of Mary Jousiffe, and Lihir Gold mine. In Kavieng, we had a Mechanical Workshop, Panelshop, Tyre service, Spare parts, Service station, Building Maintenance, and the Motor vehicle Insurance Agency. At Lihir, we had a couple of shipping containers, with a roof between them. It was not ideal, but we were not allowed to improve the temporary site we were on. Alan had unsuccessfully tried to purchase land to build a permanent workshop, but there were significant land issues and village jealousies. Getting paid for the repairs to vehicles was also a significant issue; the landowners believed they should get everything done free because the mine was on their land. We had nothing to do with the Mine, but this did not seem to matter; I eventually persuaded Alan to close down Lihir.

The business suffered greatly after *Ian Ling Stuckey* replaced Paul Tohian as Governor; Ian is a very successful businessman in his own right and brought sweeping changes to the Provincial Government. He locked the Government fleet up, Public servants no longer had a vehicle for personal use, and all new purchases made on a price basis. Local businesses no longer received priority. Regent's turn-over dropped alarmingly, as the Provincial Government had been its biggest customer by far.

We also took on the labour-intensive Agency for *Air Niugini* for one flight a day, though this was not profitable. When my second Three-year contract was due to expire, Alan decided he could no longer afford me, so I accepted a position with *"Melohn"* in Port Moresby. Malon was the first three letters of Mellisa and John, Mellisa being John's sister, she ran the company while John was working in New Ireland. Mellisa did not like me from the start, as John had employed me without her input. It was the only job in my thirty-six years in PNG that I did not enjoy.

Everyone I had talked to before I accepted the job advised me against working for Mellisa. They told me no Whitey had ever lasted a year. When I read the contract, alarm bells rang, as a large portion of the Contract graphically laid out terms for termination. If I called Mellisa any of the listed swear words explicitly detailed in the document. Previous Employees had become frustrated and vented; I thought this was not my style, so I signed the Contract.

I was the Maintenance Manager for the Real Estate units the Company owned and the Maintenance Manager for some Poker Machines in PNG. I had a crew of thirty, plumbers, carpenters, tilers, electricians, and I.T. technicians to do this. When I first arrived, Mellisa asked me if I would stand in as Manager of one of their *"Pokies Ples"* venues at Boroko, as the Philippines' manager had not turned up.

It was my first taste of the Melohn work culture, while the venue had two staff shifts. I expected to work both shifts, from eight a.m. in the morning to two a.m. the next morning, seven days a week. I was permitted to go home from seven p.m. to around eleven p.m. to get some sleep, but having my nightly sleep split into two parts was exhausting.

Margaret came and spent a couple of weeks in Port Moresby but didn't like it, and as she had a job as a Cook for Crystal trading in Kavieng, she decided to return there. Both Ephraim and Talom stayed with me, and I put them into *Ward Strip Community School*, close to where I lived. My first unit In Moresby cost K800.00 a week to rent, and while it had three bedrooms and a swimming pool, it was infested with rats and only had a cold water shower. I moved out to Boroko, where I rented another three-bedroom unit in a compound exclusively for Locals, for K450.00 a week. It was the old PTC Expatriate Compound, so the Units were comfortable.

The compound appeared to have adequate security as it had a Colorbond fence with razor wire around the top, but the gate only had a rock holding it closed. *Raskols,* never targeted the place as they concentrated on the Expatriate compounds, and I was the only white face in this one. Also, the owners were from the Highlands; they lived in the unit closest to the gate and provided around the clock security.

One Saturday morning Talom came to work with me as I was going to purchase a pair of footy boots for him; the front door security let us in. Not long after, he was marched into the venue by three *raskols,* with a gun at his head; they then switched the gun to me and ordered me to open the safe. As I worked the combination, one of them checked my pockets for cash; I had K500.00 in my trouser pocket for Talom's football boots.

Fortunately for me, as I was crouched down to open the floor-safe combination, the pocket had slipped down the side of my leg, and he did not find my money. But because he was pushing me around checking my pockets, the combination failed to open. The guy gave me a vicious kick to the head with his big boots blackening my eye; luckily for me, the safe opened the second try. Talom was held at gunpoint with the staff under the snooker table. The *raskols* fled with the money and some cigarettes. They had a stolen car and driver waiting out the front, and sped off and disappeared into *Morauta Settlement.*

When I reported the robbery to the Boss, I received no sympathy for my black eye and admonished losing the company's money, even though insured. I realised fully why the Contracts worded as they were; I could have quite easily lost my cool for the first time in PNG. Most of the National staff and the large Expatriate Philippines work-force were more sympathetic. This robbery, though, did result in the purse strings loosened a fraction to provide better security, especially on the front door. Three new doors were constructed, with patrons having the door behind them locked before the one in front was opened.

Ephraim had observed how I cooked the evening stews, and one night when I came home for my four-hour kip, he had prepared the evening meal. It was much appreciated, as before I had to cook the evening meal, which took up a large chunk of my sleep time, he became quite proficient at cooking.

A new Manager for the Poker Machine Parlour eventually turned up after three months, and I was transferred into the large tower block downtown to do my Maintenance Manager job. It was more to my liking as I only worked ten hours a day, six days a week and having Sundays off, Mellisa felt she was not getting her monies worth, having me work only sixty hours a week. As I was on Salary, she always tried to get me to work longer hours, organising work for me on Sundays and weeknights. I managed to get most Sundays off, though and would take Effie and Talom, and some of their friends to *The Airways Hotel poolside* for lunch and a swim. I would order two or three *large Pizzas* and soft drinks for the kids while I have my only drinking session for the week. It was so pleasant having a relaxing day out after working like a slave at the Pokies Venue.

My office in the Melohn Tower was the furthest away from Mellisa's Office and became the place where everyone came to have a bitch about her everyone knew they would get a sympathetic ear from me. The Accountant was a lady from the Philippines; we became good friends and reduced my tax to just a couple of hundred Kina. She did this by what seemed to be some rather dubious accounting methods. I did not complain, though, as it gave me more money to feed the ever-growing list of house guests.

Ephraim and Talom, had many friends from school, and it wasn't long before some of them who lived a long way from School were staying weeknights and then permanently. Two brothers from Popondetta, *David and Bernard,* the sons of a Pastor, became permanent guests. But seeing I spent so much time at work, I was happy my boys had many friends to keep them company. They were great kids, Bernard, in particular, would always tell me if anyone was getting into mischief, and they were happy to help around the house.

Any first time visitor would also become the target for my *"Dad Joke,"* that I had been using for years, as they were tucking into a hearty lamb stew. I would ask them if this was the first time they had eaten dog meat. The looks on their faces were priceless, the boys would tell them I was only joking, but it worked every time.

Some of the boys in the compound played AFL, and they got both Ephraim and Talom interested, so I would take them all to *Amini Park* oval on Sundays to play for the Dockers juniors. I was pleased they chose Aussie Rules instead of the more popular Rugby League, having played AFL in my younger years, in Australia and Rabaul. Both of them were quite skilful at the game, with Ephraim playing Full Forward because he was a handy overhead mark. He would wave the ball in the air like a show-pony after taking a Mark, unlike his Dad.

One night after training, the whole team walked over to my house after practice; they had no transport home. I was driving a Company Mazda ute with the Real Estate Company logo on it, but I agreed to drop them off as it was after dark. There were so many kids on the back they had to stand upright, packed like Sardines. Mellisa would have freaked out if she had seen us, but as we were going to Gerehu, a Settlement Suburb, I didn't expect to run into her. The kids in the back were singing loudly and clinging to each other grimly as we sped through the night. Pedestrians would stop and stare at the sight of twenty-five kids standing upright in the tray as the Ray White ute ran into the no go area of Gerehu. The Company must have received massive *"Street Cred"* for this, not only from the kids on the back but also from the residents who saw us. Fortunately, Mellisa never found out about this *misuse* of the Company vehicle.

At Christmas, I sent Talom and Ephraim home to Kavieng for the school holidays, and *Trevor Maino* came to spend Christmas in Moresby. Colleen also came to visit during the year, so she had trouble organising the sleeping arrangements. Colleen slept in Ephraim's room, and all the boys slept on the floor of the lounge.

Because I didn't particularly appreciate working for Melohn, I applied for a *Permanent Residency visa*, which would mean that I would not have had to be sponsored by any Company. I could do any job a PNG National could and live permanently In PNG. I had to pay K3000.00 for the application, have a Police check done and pay a further K3,000.00 for an Immigration agent to organise everything for me.

Before this Visa was approved, and after working for Monian for only fifteen months, I became ill; I put this down to the long hours and the stress of working with them. I Woke in the middle of the night and had to rush to the toilet where I haemorrhaged so much blood I went into shock, I lay in bed until morning, and the kids started stirring.

I called them in and told them they would not be going to school that day, as they would have to help me get to *Doctor Mola's private clinic*. I radioed through to work to tell them I was going to the hospital. It took me some time to get out to the car as I was blacking out, but I eventually got there and drove to the Private Hospital.

I was admitted to the Clinic, had many tests, then had bags of my blood type sent up overnight from Australia for my transfusion, as they had no A- in Moresby. Luckily I had taken some Amoxicillin antibiotics after my Haemorrhage, which had healed the area where the internal bleeding had been. One of my Techs dropped around on the orders of Mellisa to check whether the car was safe or not; I was glad to see she was true to herself and had her priorities right.

After he got all the tests results, my Haemorrhage was because of *diverticulitis*. Amoxicillin was controlling the diverticulitis. But they found I had severe Kidney disease. Originally brought on by cerebral malaria and exacerbated by consuming indomethacin anti-inflammatory tablets for gout. He asked me if I had Private medical insurance, which I didn't; he then told me I would have to return to Australia because of the *chronic kidney disease* and eventually have to rely on Kidney dialysis to survive.

When the boys came to visit in the afternoon, I told them what the Doctor had said; they were devastated, my heart ached for them. After such a rotten start in life, with their fathers not wanting to have anything to do with them. Then finally having a dad who provided everything they needed, now they were being cast adrift again. They were inconsolable; the tears flowed freely and not only from the boys. I would have taken Margaret and the whole family with me if I could have, but as our relationship was not considered official, there was no way I could have brought them to Australia. I had always planned to live out my life in Papua New Guinea, the country I loved so much and considered my home. Due to illness, my whole world turned upside down; our family that had grown so strong over the previous eight years was now going to be split-up; I was distraught.

I tried to go back to work for my notice-period but found I was exhausted by lunchtime, so I resigned straight away; I booked the kids tickets back to Kavieng and packed up my belongings, sending most of my things to *Jim King* in Kavieng. I returned to Australia with only three suitcases; I had a misguided hope that I would be cured In Australia and return home to PNG someday. Bernard and David's father and mother came to see me and thank me for my help with his family and for them to pray for my recovery. More comfort for them than for me. Bernard impressed his Mum and Dad by making tea and snacks for us as we talked.

I went to pieces when I had to take Ephraim and Talom to the Airport for their flight to Kavieng, David, Bernard, and some of the boys and girls from the compound had also come to say goodbye to them. We caused quite a scene out the front of the airport. I was very depressed later that day when It was my turn to be farewelled by the Popondetta line and friends from the compound. Thirty-six years after arriving in Port Moresby in 1970 for a one year contract with Bougainville Copper, I was finally going back, not to my home, but to a place that was like a Foreign Country to me.

Leaving all my friends and loved ones behind in PNG, I experienced massive culture shock returning to Australia. I had to retrieve my passport from PNG Immigration before my Permanent Residency Visa was issued. The Visa was approved a few months after I arrived in Australia.

I did not enjoy my flight back to Cairns and found Australia had changed so much since I had left. I had trouble settling into the very selfish white lifestyle of a somewhat racist redneck country.

THE END

Printed in the United States
by Baker & Taylor Publisher Services